Community & Conflict
A Study of French-English Relations in Ontario

John D. Jackson
Concordia University

Canadian Scholars' Press Inc.   **Toronto**   **1994**

Community and Conflict

First published in 1988 by
Canadian Scholars' Press Inc.
180 Bloor St. W., Ste. 402,
Toronto, Ontario   M5S 2V6
Reprinted in 1994.

Canadian Cataloguing in Publication Data

Main entry under title:

Jackson, John D.

Rev. ed.
Bibliography: p.
ISBN 0-921627-22-X

1. Canada — English-French relations — Case Studies.
2. Tecumseh (Ont.) — Ethnic relations — Case studies.
3. Social conflict — Ontario — Case studies. I. Title.

FC3100.5.J32   1988   305.7'09713'31   C88-093333-X
F1059.7.F83J32   1988

Printed and bound in Canada

1975 Preface

This book was written with two thoughts in mind. As an Anglophone Quebecer, I was curious to know about and to understand the situation of Francophones living outside of and some distance from Quebec. As a sociologist, I was interested in the way in which people, in the course of their daily lives, cope with social movements that are national in scope and have considerable historical depth. I believe that the concrete manifestations of French-English relations are to be found at the local level where people interact in the neighbourhood, in the church and parish, in the schools, and in political institutions in terms of their membership in one or the other category. This is a case study of one community. It is my hope that the paradigm proposed for the analysis of community conflict will stimulate comparative studies to complete the picture.

I have placed considerable weight on the ways in which people at the local level organize to deal with conflicts that are programmed for continuation. In doing so, I have stressed the processes that lead to an institutionalization or a regulation of conflicts. I would ask the reader to keep in mind that in the long run the regulation of a conflict between a dominant and subordinate party is to the advantage of the former. To remain intact or to grow, a minority party must constantly challenge the mechanisms that regulate conflict and preserve the peace.

J.D.J.
Montreal, April 1975

Preface 1987

This second edition of the Tecumseh study appears twenty-three years after the original research and twelve years after its publication. In the meantime, language as a symbol of the relations between Quebec and Canada and French and English speakers throughout Canada has remained paramount in Canadian life. Largely because of the federal pan-Canadian policy on French/English bilingualism, the question has revolved around the "official language minorities" — Francophones outside of Quebec and Anglophones in Quebec.

In response, since 1975 several hundred monographs and articles have appeared extending the issues raised in the 1964-66 Tecumseh research. To name but a few, the reader will find that the following complement this publication: in 1977 several papers given at a conference sponsored by the Canada Council on "The Individual, Language and Society" were published under the editorship of W.H. Coons et al; Danielle Juteau and Jean Lapointe have reported extensively on research conducted in the Ottawa Valley and Northern Ontario (e.g., see Juteau-Lee and Lapointe: 1978); and Sheila McLeod-Arnopoulos' *Voices from French Ontario* (1982) provides an excellent overview of the question in Ontario. Caldwell and Waddell's *The English of Quebec* (1982) and Rudin's *The Forgotten Quebecers* (1985) will give the reader insight into the history and problems of Anglophones in Quebec.

The two issues upon which the Tecumseh study focused — French-English and Protestant-Catholic relations — have again surfaced in public debate in Ontario. In the summer of 1984 William Davis, then Premier of Ontario, announced the extension of full-funding to separate schools for grades eleven through thirteen. This action became a major issue in the provincial elections of 1985. A few months later, in November 1986, the newly constituted Ontario legislature under Premier David Peterson passed Bill 8 extending French language services in the province. Bill 8 became a major issue in the 1987 elections.

Thus does a second edition of *Community & Conflict* provide background to the current shape of the debate, a background which gives the reader a sense of how these issues affect the everyday life of people in towns and villages across the country. There is another reason. The community studies tradition has been sadly neglected, with notable exceptions, in Canadian sociology (it has continued to be reasonably strong in anthropology) perhaps because of an assumed eclipse of small town life as a consequence of urbanization and centralization. This is in spite of the fact that movement into metropolitan centres has stabilized and that one-fifth of the population reside in centres under 10,000 — centres which have exhibited growth into the eighties (Hodge & Qadeer, 1984). It is in these small centres that close to six million people live out their daily lives partly structured by the local situation and partly by regional and national events.

On the question of the linkages between local, regional and national systems, the reader is invited to examine a critique of the Tecumseh study by Alex Stewart published in *Canadian Ethnic Studies* (1980). Among the several interesting and valid points regarding my interpretation of the data, he questioned the suitability of applying a model derived from the societal level (i.e., the elite accommodation model of French-English relations) to the local or community level of interaction. My response, a position to which I still hold, was to note that the basic question in community studies must be directed toward specific local articulations with particular configurations of economic, political-legal and ideological elements underlying the social life of particular societies at particular times. This allows for local variations and rhythms on a "national" theme while avoiding the error that locale is somehow independent of the society of which it is a part.

The people of Tecumseh did not invent the categories of French Catholic, English Catholic, or English Protestant as used in this study, nor did they wholly invent the social meanings inherent in these categories. The categories and their shifting meanings were a part of the population's political and ideological heritage, a part which they molded to yield an understanding of local and national events. The materials which they used to so structure their lives was a combination of local, provincial and national experience through time.

In the preparation of this second edition there was a temptation to rewrite the entire text. However, to have done so would have required new research. This is a revision. The original data has neither been changed nor extended. Corrections have been made and, where appropriate, 1981 census data was added. In the main, the picture presented is that of Tecumseh in 1966 and 1973. The most difficult editing task was to remove the sexist bias from the original study. It has been removed from the text, but insofar as it was built into the analysis of the 1964-66 sample, the picture as derived from these data remains that of male life in the community.

J.D.J.
Montreal, December 1, 1987

Acknowledgements

A project of the type reported here involves many people over a long period of time. The citizens of Tecumseh in all walks of life and of both language groups were exceptionally helpful and very interested in my work. There were a few who contributed considerably to my understanding of the community and who opened their hearts, their homes, and their day-to-day lives to the inquiring and perhaps overly curious stranger in their midst. I would like to name each, but to do so would break confidentiality. To them and their co-citizens, my heartfelt thanks. My one hope is that the pages to follow do justice to their community.

There are some who can be named. I would like to thank Professor Rudolf Helling of the University of Windsor for his help during the fieldwork period. I would also like to recognize the assistance of Professor Walter Freeman, formerly of Michigan State University, and Professor James B. McKee of that university. Many others contributed at a later date. My thanks are also extended to Professor Frank Vallee of Carleton University for many hours spent discussing the issues raised in this book. William Smith, Nancy Smith, John McMullan, and Paul Millen provided bibliographic assistance. Elva Jackson acted as research assistant, critic, and typist throughout the duration of the project.

A good deal of the funds necessary for a project like this were provided by the Canada Council through a doctoral fellowship in 1965 and a leave fellowship in 1972.

To the people of Tecumseh

Ceux qui vivent ce sont ceux qui luttent.
Ceux dont l'âpres destin remplit l'âme et le coeur...
Victor Hugo

Table of Contents

Chapter One

Conflict and Harmony

Perspectives

It is not a sin against science to admit that there are a wide variety of perspectives on any issue and that complete objectivity is virtually impossible. Experiences are never perceived in their raw state either by the participants or by observers. Everyone tends to interpret events through previous concepts and experiences. Conceptualization is a process of generalization and selection (McKinney, 1966, p. 9). Selection is the key word. Experience is ordered through a selection of those aspects which have meaning in relation to our cultural heritage, social position, personal history, and immediate objectives. This could be taken a step further with the statement that the range of available perspectives or selection devices is a function of the historical period in which the investigator lives. A given perspective highlights certain aspects of what we experience, but neglects or ignores others. The perspective that one assumes will, therefore, generate different questions and, ultimately, different answers about reality. Basically, there are two major conceptions of "community." Robert Nisbet in *The Quest for Community* is concerned with primary relationships. This involves concepts of "integration, status, membership, hierarchy, symbol, norm, identification, group" which are related to the notion of *Gemeinschaft*-like relationships (Nisbet 1953, pp. 23, 49). These are relationships "of concord based upon bonds of blood (kinship), place (neighbourhood), or mind (friendship)" (McKinney 1966, p. 103). The second conception of community emphasizes place or locality. This perspective views settlements, towns, villages or cities as communities. In the latter case we are referring to "the community" as a place, in contrast with the former case in which "community" is seen as a particular type of interaction (Bernard 1973, pp. 3-5). As might be expected, the definition of "community" becomes a

1

component in definitions of "the community," but the emphasis is on concord, cohesiveness and order. One can see, then, how easily conflict, disorganization, disintegration and disharmony become antithetical to "the community."

In this study, I shall deal with "the community" as a locality, and take conflict to be a form of human interaction that exists side by side with harmonious interaction. To be sure, conflict may well contribute to the disintegration of certain existing relationships within the community. On the other hand, it may contribute to the strengthening of certain relationships while weakening others, or it may contribute to the building of new relationships while breaking down a particular status quo.

In dealing with French-English relationships at the local level I am admitting that locality-based relationships continue to be of social significance and an important focus of study. This is stated in spite of my awareness that the autonomy and independence of the community is declining. It will therefore be necessary to take the current trends from community to society, from autonomy to dependence, and from independence to interdependence into account. However, conflicts of the type considered in this study focus on concrete issues at the local level. The question is, therefore, where and by whom are the decisions affecting the outcomes of such issues made. With the growing participation of regional, provincial and federal decision-making machinery in local matters, the likelihood of local issues being settled solely within the community is extremely low.

The concepts of vertical and horizontal patterns of organization will provide a useful means of dealing with this problem. A community's vertical pattern has been defined as "the structural and functional relations of its various social units and sub-systems to extra-community systems" (Warren 1963, p. 161). Horizontal patterns are "the structural and functional relations of [the community's] various social units and sub-systems to each other" (Warren 1963, p. 162). For example an issue over language in a local school may be mediated within the horizontal pattern drawing only a local parents' association and school board into play or it may move into the vertical pattern bringing the provincial Department of Education into the picture.

2

We have now established that our inquiry will be based upon a particular perspective. That perspective will be one which views communities as locally based interaction systems; focuses on conflict as one form of interaction; and considers the regional, provincial and national ties between external and internal systems. Now we may proceed with a short description of what is meant by conflict, whether it occurs on the personal or group level, and what the conflict is over.

Conflict

Who is in Conflict with Whom?

In studies of conflict, it is very important to specify the units of analysis. In any social setting one may examine conflict between individuals (interpersonal conflict), conflict among individuals in groups (intragroup conflict), or conflict between groups as groups (intergroup conflict). Each type calls for different data and different analytical tools. Unfortunately, it is all too common for generalizations about intergroup conflict to be made from propositions derived from interpersonal and intragroup conflict. Although people involved in conflicts do act both as individuals and as members of a group, this does not mean that intergroup behaviour can be explained as a case of interpersonal or intragroup conflict.

In this study, I shall adopt a social realist orientation and attempt to look at events as instances of intergroup or social conflict.[1] The task, therefore, will be to examine the collective base from which conflicts arise. The struggle of Franco-Ontarians to gain status in a world dominated by Anglophones and to extend the use of their language in an officially declared bilingual setting will be looked at not as the result of disgruntled malcontents or hot-heads, but as the result of a struggle

---

1. Social realism holds that entities like groups, institutions, elements of social structure, etc., are other than or above and beyond the individuals acting them out (Gould and Kolb 1964, p. 665). The point is, both the "person" of individual psychology and the "group" of sociology are abstractions; neither are concrete entities. However, "the group is understandable and explicable...in terms of distinctly social processes and factors, not by reference to individual psychology" (Warriner 1956, p. 550).

for status and identification emerging from their *particular positions and roles in the social system.*

Intergroup Conflict

The word "group" is commonly used to refer to just about any collection of people or things. Families are called groups, but so is a crowd gathered around a fire down the street. The five or six ten-year-olds who regularly play together are called a group, but so is the morning school assembly. Clearly, these are not identical phenomena; there should be either a different term for each or, perhaps, one should speak of different types of groups. To deal adequately with intergroup conflict, the term "group" must be defined more precisely than its everyday usage.

The collection of people gathered at a bus stop with nothing in common but their presence on the same spot at the same time would best be referred to as an *aggregate.* An aggregate is simply a collection of people with no relationships obtaining among them and with no shared property of social significance. A *statistical category* is also another kind of collection of people without relationships among the members. There is, however, a specified property held in common. Census categories like "ethnic origin," "mother tongue," "sex" and so on, are statistical categories. For example, an examination of the 1971 Census figures for Cornwall would indicate that there were 18,165 people whose mother tongue was French. Unless one had gathered additional evidence, there is nothing in the census itself to permit one to assume that this collection of people is anything but a statistical category. All that is known is that each of these people learned French first and still understands the language. That is the definition of "mother tongue" (Census 1972, p. 26).

Continuing with the above example, a rudimentary knowledge of Canadian history would suggest the hypothesis that there may well be some level of relationship among the 18,165 people in Cornwall whose mother tongue is French. One would not be far wrong in assuming that, at a minimum, there is a vague sense of membership or identity and a minimum capacity for collective action. If this were the case, then the collection would more appropriately be labelled a *social category*. Occupational groupings, social classes, and age groupings are frequently social categories. However, not all statistical categories are social categories, nor does it follow that statistical categories can become social categories.

A fully developed *collectivity* would be the final step along the path of increasing identification and level of interaction. The presence of a collectivity implies:

> (1) a distinctive culture; (2) tests or criteria of membership; (3) a set of constitutive norms regulating social relations both within the collectivity and with outsiders; (4) an awareness of distinct identity by both members and nonmembers; (5) obligations of solidarity; ...and (6) a high capacity for continued action by the collectivity on behalf of its members or of itself as a unit.
>
> (Williams 1964, p.18)

At a minimum, therefore, intergroup conflict would require two or more social categories. Indeed as we shall see, conflict, by promoting ingroup solidarity, can stimulate a collection of people to increase their interaction and identify with each other to the point where they move from the level of social category to collectivity.

Before we can discuss intergroup conflict, it is necessary to demonstrate empirically that the categories of people about which this study is concerned are more than mere aggregates or statistical categories. It will also be necessary to demonstrate that there is interaction among them as social categories or *conflict parties*.

Social conflict is, after all, a form of interaction that requires the parties to be in communication with each other. Conflict requires community (Dahrendorf 1959, p. 225). This may appear to be a paradox, but only if it is assumed that harmony is a necessary property of communities.

5

Conflict Over What?

To state the obvious, conflicts take place over something. Incompatible values, and/or position and resource scarcity would summarize the conditions that must be present for conflict relations to obtain among two or more social categories or collectivities (Mack and Snyder 1957, pp. 212-248). A condition of position scarcity arises when, for example, desirable positions in the social structure are distributed in such a manner that the members of one particular social category are underrepresented and another overrepresented. The underrepresentation of Francophones compared to Anglophones in higher-status occupations is a well documented fact of Canadian life (Porter 1965, pp. 91-98).

Resource scarcity is a question of supply and demand; each social category or collectivity in a two-party conflict cannot have all they want of desirable objects or "states of affairs" (Mack and Snyder 1957, p. 218). An example of a simple form of this condition is when representatives of Francophone interests in a local Ontario school system fight for a greater share of the budget for special programs within their sphere of responsibility. Decisions about the distribution of resources must then be made according to collective interests and claims as well as according to pedagogical principles. However, not only money and material goods are involved in this category of resources. Prestige (or social status) is also a resource that may be unequally distributed according to membership in various social categories. French as a language is accorded less prestige than English in public life in Ontario. A good deal of the struggle of Franco-Ontarians is over the prestige accorded their language in schools and other spheres of public activity.

Empirically, it is difficult to conceive of a pure value conflict. Incompatible values are usually compounded with position and resource scarcity. The separation is, however, analytically useful. It enables one to examine the manner in which contradictory value positions are related to position and resource scarcity. In this study, the two major parties, Francophones and Anglophones, assume incompatible positions on assimilation. Complete assimilation and complete separation are incompatible; one is the contradiction of the other. Each party tends to move toward one or the other extreme; Francophones toward the latter, Anglophones toward the former. The actual state is one of pluralism. The issue is just how much separation is to be *demanded* (from a Francophone point of view) or how much is to be *permitted* (from an Anglophone point of view).

One seldom finds conflict situations initially or overtly about status differentials or incompatible values. Conflict episodes, as we observe them, initially take place over specific and tangible issues. These issues, in the course of mediation, draw underlying values and status differentials into play.

Vertical and Horizontal Patterns

Conflict between Francophones and Anglophones is a national issue. It finds its concrete expressions at all levels of Canadian life, federal, provincial and municipal. Communities respond differently to provincial legislation according to their location, to demographic variables, and to the strength of local horizontal patterns of organization. At a more general level, local conflicts over language rights, whether they occur in New Brunswick (Moncton), Quebec (St-Léonard), Ontario (Cornwall), or Manitoba (St. Boniface), cannot be understood without reference to the role the provinces play in the language question, to the British North America Act and, indeed, to the meaning of Confederation.

In this way, a local conflict involves not only local, provincial and federal organizations and governments, but must also be seen in its historical perspective. As we saw, very few conflicts are overtly about differences in status or values, but these are often drawn into the conflict. In order fully to comprehend the particular issue, it is therefore necessary to take a much wider historical perspective.

Tecumseh, Ontario

This book is based upon research done in Tecumseh, a small Ontario town with a sizable proportion of Franco-Ontarians. The research focused on conflict between linguistic groups and the manner in which people deal with these conflicts at the local level. In addition to language, religion was also taken into account as a category with social significance. The study, therefore, dealt with conflicts among three categories of people: French-speaking Roman Catholics, English-speaking Roman Catholics and English-speaking Protestants.

Tecumseh, a town of some 5000 people, is located in Essex County on the eastern boundary of the city of Windsor. It is in the heartland of the automotive industry and eastern Canada's manufacturing belt. In 1961, Essex County accounted for 49 percent of the value of factory shipments in the Lake St. Clair region (Ontario 1967, p. 61). Along with Windsor, Tecumseh is a border town. A glance at the map will show that the Windsor district is closer in driving time to Detroit, Toledo, and Cleveland than to Toronto.

Essex County is the one county in southwestern Ontario with a significant proportion of residents whose mother tongue is French. The combined population of Essex and Kent Counties whose mother tongue is French amounted to 9 percent of the total population in 1961. Though this had dropped somewhat by 1971, these two counties contain the major French-speaking communities in southwestern Ontario. Most French-speakers in the region are in Windsor and the small communities along the southern shores of Lake St. Clair, including Tecumseh. Tables 1 and 2 show the religious and ethnic composition of Tecumseh from 1921 to 1981. The trend toward an increasingly larger proportion of anglophones in the population is obvious, even taking into account that the severe drop in the proportion of francophones between 1971 and 1981 was influenced by the new "multiple origins" catagory.

The Selection of Tecumseh

Tecumseh was not originally selected in order to pursue studies in social conflict. The initial interest was in the problem of assimilation and the viability of Francophone communities outside the Province of Quebec. The conflict model was introduced after initial observations in the community.

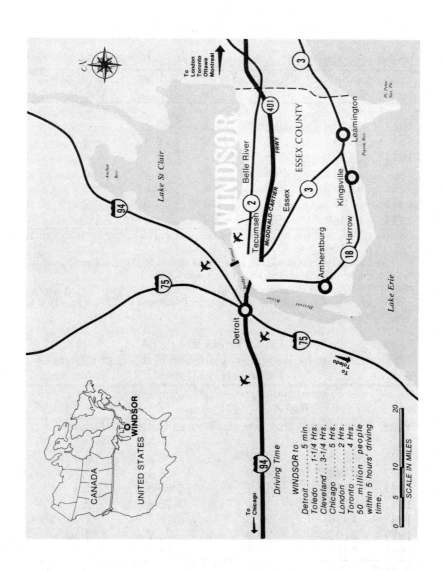

Table 1
Distribution by Ethnic Origin of the
Population of Tecumseh, 1921-1981

Percentage Distribution According to Ethnic Origin

Year	Population	British	French	Other	Multiple Origins[a]
1921	978	10.5	86.3	3.2	—
1931	2129	18.6	74.6	6.8	—
1941	2412	20.6	74.1	5.3	—
1951	3543	26.6	63.3	10.1	—
1961	4476	30.3	55.9	13.8	—
1971	5105	37.9	47.6	14.5	—
1981	6385[b]	39.8	33.8	14.4	12.0

Source: Census of Canada; Vol. 1, 1921; Vol. 2, 1931; Vol. 2, 1941; Vol. 1, 1951; Vol. 1, 1961; Vol. 1, 1971; Vol. 3, 1981.

[a]A new catagory, "Multiple Origins," was added to the 1981 census to allow for combinations of British, French and Other

[b]Population figures for geographic areas differ in reports utilizing sample data. The official population reported for Tecumseh in 1971 was 5165; in 1981, 6364.

Table 2
Distribution by Religious Affiliation of the Population of
Tecumseh, 1921-1981

Percentage Distribution According to Religious Affiliation

Year	Population	Protestant	Roman Catholic	Other
1921	978	6.2	93.8	0.0
1931	2129	10.9	88.4	0.7
1941	2412	11.7	86.9	1.4
1951	3543	18.2	79.8	2.0
1961	4476	21.3	76.7	2.0
1971	5105	22.0	74.7	3.2
1981	6385	20.5	75.2	4.3

Source: Census of Canada; Vol. 1, 1921; Vol. 2, 1931; Vol. 2, 1941; Vol. 1, 1951; Vol. 1, 1961; Vol. 1, 1971; Vol. 3, 1981.

Conflict & Harmony

Given the region in which Tecumseh is located, the continuing existence of a Francophone community is quite surprising. The fact that the community is diminishing in size and activity is not so surprising. In this respect, the selection of Tecumseh was not an accident. My initial interest was in the kind of social milieu that can maintain a French-speaking community in spite of the weight of factors working against it. These factors are not difficult to find. Essex County is isolated from Quebec, the mainstream of French culture in North America. It is equally isolated from the Ottawa Valley and northeastern Ontario, the Francophone strong-holds in Ontario. In addition, there is the overwhelming influence of the United States, especially in this part of Ontario. If the population whose mother tongue was French accounted for 10 percent of Windsor's population in 1961, it would represent only 1 to 2 percent of the total population of the Windsor-Detroit metropolis (Joy 1972, p. 33). The Windsor region's proximity to the United States cannot be ignored. Economically, Windsor is a branch plant for Detroit.

Apart from the desire to examine the viability of a French-speaking community with overwhelming odds against its continued existence, there was another reason for selecting Tecumseh. Tecumseh is urban and industrialized. Most community studies concerned with French Canada have been conducted in rural regions. In fact, to many Anglophones, the *habitant*, the rural farmer, is the stereotype of a French Canadian. The rural community has been presented as representative of French-Canadian social organization, but one only need pursue the history of the French in North America to discover the fallacy of this assertion (Garigue 1960, pp. 181 -201).

There were also personal reasons for selecting Tecumseh, if I may be permitted to introduce non-scientific criteria. I grew up in a town outside Montreal, just as Tecumseh is outside Windsor. As an Anglophone in Quebec, I had the privilege of a unilingual English school system from grade one through to university graduation. The French-speakers of Tecumseh have not had the same privilege. Ultimately, it was my intention to compare the position of a French minority in Ontario to an English minority in Quebec, though this objective will not be pursued here.

Methods of Data Collection

Five techniques of collecting data were used during the course of the research: participant observation, in-depth interviewing of selected respondents, analysis of selected documents, and a structured questionnaire administered to a random sample drawn from the 1965 municipal voters' list. Each of these will be described briefly. However, an overview of the total process should provide a useful perspective on the research. The work proceeded in three stages. Observation and unstructured interviewing were the principal methods employed in the first two stages; structured interviewing and the questionnaire were used during the third stage.

During the spring and fall of 1964, I made several trips to Tecumseh in order to assess the community's suitability as a research site. I also examined the structure of the community, paying particular attention to linguistic and religious categories, and the significance these categories had for social interaction within the community. The second stage began in May, 1965 when I took up residence in the community. The period of residence ended in July, 1966. For an eight-month period, until January, 1966, extensive observation and interviewing took place. The third stage, from January to July, 1966, was devoted to an analysis of previously collected data followed by structured interviewing and the administration of the questionnaire. Most of the material used here was collected during 1965 and 1966. I made a brief second trip to Tecumseh during the spring of 1972 to discover what changes had taken place during the six-year interval and to update the material.[2]

Observation

The problems inherent in participant observation are well documented (Cicourel 1964; Bruyn 1966; Vidich 1964). The principal danger lies in the difficulty in maintaining sufficient controls and checks on the data collected in this manner to en-

2. The author wishes to acknowledge the support received from the Canada Council during the initial research and for the period devoted to the writing of this manuscript.

sure reliability and validity. A major source of control is the observer's cognizance of the procedures employed, the accurate recording of these procedures, and their effects upon himself or herself and the study subjects. To this end, the observer must keep four questions in mind. What role or roles are assumed in the field and for what purpose? What should be observed? What procedures should be used to record observations? What procedures should be used to maintain checks on the data? (Selltiz 1959, p. 205).

I assumed several roles in the field. I was never a "complete participant" in the sense of being intensely involved with the study subjects in day-to-day situations without their knowledge of my research objectives. At times, in restaurants, taverns and various public meetings and events, I did interact with those present without their knowledge of my identity or purpose. Data gathered in these situations were used to provide a feeling for the total community. More often I adopted a "participant-as-observer" role. Here, the stress was on participation, but the respondents were aware of my objectives. I found myself playing this role with increasing frequency as the fieldwork progressed and I was becoming more widely known. Later, I adopted an "observer-as-participant" role in the many associational meetings and public events I attended. Here I was accepted and recognized as an observer, but participation was neither expected nor desired.[3] These various styles of observation yielded the basic data for analysis and each helped to provide a check on the other.

Interviewing

Two types of interviewing were used. The first, an unstructured type, was employed throughout all phases of the research. The second, a more structured type, was used during the final phase. The first type is referred to as "unstructured" because identical sets of predetermined questions were not

---

3. The categories of complete participant, participant-as-observer, and observer-as-participant are defined and discussed in an article by Raymond L. Gold, "Roles in Sociological Field Observations," *Social Forces* 36 (March, 1958).

administered to each respondent. Some of these interviews were *focused* in that an appointment was made with a respondent to discuss a specific issue or issues which had arisen during the course of observations made in the community. Others were *non-directive* in that there was no particular focus, and the initiative in the interview was left largely to the respondent. A total of seventy-two unstructured interviews were conducted.

In contrast, structured interviews made use of a standard set of questions administered to each respondent. Six different interview schedules were used to obtain data on a variety of items concerning associations in the community, provincial and regional associations, and evidence concerning conflict relations. Respondents were selected from a number of associations and key positions in the community. A total of forty-one interviews of this type were conducted.

Documents

Documentary analysis involved the use of newspapers and associational records. Four area newspapers were used, covering a period from 1931 to 1965. My interest was in reported events, cross-checked with other sources, and editorial opinion. The minutes and correspondence of four Tecumseh-based voluntary associations were submitted to content analysis.

Questionnaire and Sample

Toward the end of the third phase, a standardized fixed-alternative questionnaire was administered to a sample of Tecumseh residents. The questionnaire was in both French and English. French-speaking respondents were assigned to bilingual interviewers. A word about the sample would be useful at this point. A population of 1177 households was selected from the 1965 municipal voters' list after those on the list not residing in Tecumseh and those who did not qualify under the definition of "household" had been eliminated. From this population, a simple random sample of 224 households was drawn using a table of random numbers. The sample used in the analysis consisted of 167 units, representing three-quarters of the original 224 units, and 14.2 percent of the total population.

These various techniques for collecting data were not selected at random. Each was related to a specific research objective and these objectives were tied to the questions discussed earlier in the chapter. It was not accidental that structured interviewing and the administration of the questionnaire took place toward the conclusion of the research period. It would have been hazardous to construct interview schedules and questionnaires without a thorough knowledge of the history of French-English relations and a sense of the meanings that local residents attached to those patterns which had developed in their community. This was where participant observation and unstructured interviewing served a special purpose. I was able to experience, at least to a certain extent, the subjective dimension of the situation studied before compiling the questionnaire.

The Procedure

In this chapter, a few general questions were raised and a conceptual framework presented. The general objective is to understand how and why people respond as they do in the course of their everyday tasks to conflicts that are national in scope and carry considerable historical depth.

Tecumseh is but one community. Nevertheless, the fact of French-English relations affects the things people do in this town to a considerable degree. How you vote in municipal, provincial and federal elections, the kind of schooling your children receive, the church you attend and the organizations you join in that church, the language you use and where you use that language, and a host of other events related to daily life at the local level are affected, in one way or another, by the history of the relationships between Francophones and Anglophones in Canada. Accordingly, in Chapter 2, I will briefly examine the history of French-English relations and try to determine the meaning of the categories French and English. From here, we will take a look at the Francophone population outside Quebec and examine the two major issues with which we will be concerned in Tecumseh — French and Catholic schooling in Ontario.

Chapters 3 and 4 focus on Tecumseh, its people and its institutions. A major objective in these two chapters is to demonstrate the presence of social categories based on language and religion, the meaning attached to these categories, and their implication for social interaction. In Chapter 5, we will look at these categories as conflict parties and the ways in which conflict is structured in relation to the roles of individuals and associations. The dynamics of the relationships among the conflict parties are examined in Chapter 6. Here I will analyze the issues over which confrontations have taken place and the mechanisms which have evolved to enable the parties to relate to each other. Finally, in Chapter 7, we return to our original questions and conceptual framework, refining the scheme in the light of our research in Tecumseh.

Chapter Two

The French-English Fact

The debate whether Canada is uninational or binational; unilingual or bilingual; unicultural, bicultural or multicultural will never end while both French and English remain together within the framework of a single state. Whatever the prevailing interpretations might be, the fact remains that a significant proportion of Canada's population is divided into two categories, French and English. Moreover, wherever and whenever people come into contact with each other on the basis of their membership in these categories, the legacy of superordinate-subordinate relationships of conflict and accomodation weighs heavily.

Anglophones and Francophones do not face each other in Tecumseh in an historical or political vacuum. Men and women not only make their own history, they carry the burden of the past with them. A knowledge of the historical background enables one to appreciate the implicit meanings of many of the observed reactions in contacts between the two linguistic groups. For this reason, it will be necessary to set the historical context within which French-English relations in Tecumseh took place.

The French Fact

The French fact or *le fait français* is a fairly common phrase in discussions of French-English relations. The important point is not, however, the *French* fact, but the relationship between French and English. The phrase would have no meaning if a Francophone people did not exist within a largely Anglophone state. The notion of a French fact is very easily translated into the notion of a "French problem," but there would be no French problem if there were no English. More than three decades ago, Everett C. Hughes noted that:

the relations [among ethnic groups] can be no more understood by studying one or the other of the groups than can a chemical combination by study of one element only, or a boxing bout by observation of only one of the fighters.
(Hughes and Hughes 1952, p. 158)

In spite of this admonition, a good deal of the sociology of inter- group relations deals with only one of the groups involved, usually the minority.

If there is a problem, it does not lie within one or the other group as a separate entity, but in the fact that the two groups are living together. The relationship that must command our attention is that between the two collectivities, and it must be remembered that this relationship has developed in a particular setting and with a particular history.

A Brief History of the French-English Fact

Within the limits of this study, we shall examine the French-English fact from the point of view of Anglophone assimilation policies versus the Francophone quest for survival in a hostile milieu. Obviously we are dealing with contacts between two peoples or nationalities. Not so obvious is the impact on future relations of the form and content of the initial contact experience.

Contact situations can be divided into two basic types (Lieberson 1961, p. 903). The first is that in which an indigenous ethnic, national or racial group subordinates a migrant population. Though not unique to North America, this is the type of contact situation with which North Americans are most familiar. Migrating populations become "ethnic minorities" to the dominant or superordinate white, Anglo-Saxon, Protestant population, the "host society." With some notable exceptions, the decision to migrate is voluntary. In addition, it is individuals or, at best, families who migrate, not whole societies. The new immigrant, though he/she may find some institutional support within his/her own group, eventually tends to become a part of the host society. The probability that the concept of a nation within a nation would develop from this type of contact situation is very low.

In contrast, the second type of contact is where an indigenous population is subordinated by an incoming population. In this case, the subordination is usually achieved through conquest. The subordination of native North American populations by Europeans would be an example; and so would the subordination of the population of New France by the British. The important aspect of this type of contact for our analysis is that it takes the form of a clash between total societies; one society succeeds in dominating another. The end result is not that of the immigrant who must adjust to the chosen place of migration, but that of a peace which must be negotiated between two antagonists. Though the average English-speaking Canadian persists in viewing French-speaking co-citizens as an ethnic group within the framework of the first type of contact situation, the fact remains that the relations between the two are a consequence of the second type of contact situation.

By the time of the conquest, New France had had two and a quarter centuries to develop into a well-established and self-conscious society. The indigenous subordinate group possessed a fully developed society with its institutions and a way of life peculiar to those institutions and the surrounding environment. The incoming superordinate group was thus required to deal with established structures.

Their first act was to negotiate a peace. The conquest was not a clear-cut victory, and the incoming group, the British, held their position by virtue of a treaty negotiated at the metropolitan rather than the local level. In order to maintain its hold on the territory, the colonial administration had little choice but to recognize the new subordinate group and reach an accommodation.

In dealing with two-party conflict there is always a danger in assuming that an accommodation is achieved through a simple linear link between the two parties. This, of course, is not the case. Each party has a social organization of its own, with its internal patterns of dominance and submission based on class, status, and power. An accommodation must therefore be reached between the different parts of each society. In a typical colonial case, the elite of the subordinate party is permitted and encouraged to maintain its dominance over its own under classes, thereby providing an effective control for the superordinate party.

Like other societies in the mid-eighteenth century, New France was in transition from feudalism to capitalism and, within capitalism itself, from a mercantile to a manufacturing society (Ryerson 1963, p. 149). In addition, the state and the Church, the aristocrats and the bourgeoisie, both local and metropolitan, were divided in various and often-changing alliances (Wade 1955, p. 5; Clark 1962, p. 20; Ryerson 1963, pp. 147-164).

Following the capitulation of Quebec and Montreal, the metropolitan authority of France, some merchants and some of the leading seigneurs returned to Europe, whereas the rural and urban lower classes, the majority of the seigneurs, and the clergy remained in New France (Brunet 1964, p. 57). The secular side of French authority was effectively destroyed. It remained for the Church and seigneurs to work out an accommodation with the new rulers. One state authority had simply replaced another.[1] However, as the new colonial administrators were practically all military officers and government officials, and therefore tended to be Tory and feudal in outlook, they were sympathetic to the goals of the French clergy and seigneurs (Lower 1958). This was to be of some significance in the future.

The early officials of the British regime were not intent on developing a commercial empire as the French servants of Louis XIV had been. The status of these officials in their own society and their attachment to the established Church of England enabled them better to understand and sympathize with the goals of French Catholicism. With this background, they found themselves in open conflict with their own merchant class.

---

1. A debate continues as to just who and how many left following the conquest. Whether the society of New France was decapitated or not and whether fundamental structural changes occurred or not, the fact remains that the conquest imposed a new "Anglo-colonial ruling class on the conquered French-Canadian nation" (Ryerson 1963, p. 205; Ouellet 1962, p.428, Brunet 1964).

The French-English Fact

The interests of the French *habitants* and incipient working class, temporarily at least, coincided with their English-speaking neighbours to the south. Though on a purely national basis, the French were subordinate to the English, settlers and merchants, whether French or English, opposed Church, seigneurs, and administrators. At another level, settlers, as an incipient working class, opposed a largely English merchant class.

It is clear that a view of the situation solely in terms of nationality obscures the nature of the relationships between the two peoples. The simple "race-relations cycle" model applied to immigrant and host society does not hold.[2] Underlying relationships based on social class intersected with relationships based on nationality and religion. Alliances among the elites of both groups served to strengthen their independent existence as nationalities and prevent the complete assimilation of the subordinate population.

Because of these complexities, and because of the growing rebellion to the south, the administration pursued an active policy of encouraging the loyalty and support of the French clergy and seigneurs. The Quebec Act of 1774 cemented the alliance between the British colonial rulers and the French elite. In effect, the French community in Canada became a recognized entity and early hopes of assimilation were delayed.

With the influx of English settlers after the American Revolution, French-speaking citizens of the colony found themselves, for the first time, face-to-face with a significant number of English-speakers. The creation of Upper and Lower Canada by the Constitutional Act of 1791 effectively separated the two linguistic communities, thereby strengthening their separate identities. It also served to abort a democratic revolution based on a class alliance crossing the linguistic lines. English and French supporters of the 1835-38 rebellions were never able to form an effective alliance.

---

2. The "race-relations cycle" refers to a statement by Robert Park to the effect that a cycle of "contacts, competition, accommodation, and eventual assimilation is apparently progressive and irreversible" (Park 1964, p. 150). This statement has provided a basic orientation in several studies on race and ethnic relations.

In spite of the subsequent efforts the British made in 1840 to reintroduce assimilation policies, the dual conflicts between the social classes and the two nationalities continued. The contingencies faced by colonial policy makers on the one hand and the fact that the French, though in a subordinate position, held sufficient numerical power to force compromises, served further to institutionalize the two linguistic communities.

Confederation: An Alternate Accommodation

The British North America Act of 1867 establishing the Dominion of Canada was partly brought about by the two interweaving processes of "industrial capitalist development" and the interaction between two "distinct national communities" (Ryerson 1968, pp. 358-359). These correspond to the class and national questions we have been discussing.

After 107 years of contact, the French and English, though still in a superordinate-subordinate relationship, were now recognized and legitimized as separate parties. The minority was never absorbed by the majority and, indeed, political and economic contingencies promoted the development of the minority community, although in a subordinate position. French and English Canada faced each other in 1867 as distinctly recognizable collectivities. Confederation was yet another possible mechanism by which the two could maintain the relationship.

Underlying the national issue was the development of industrial capitalism. The colonies were emerging from mercantilism into an industrial stage. The old alliance between French clergy and seigneur and English colonial administrator shifted to an alliance between French clergy and business elite and the English-Canadian bourgeoisie. The alliance which had enabled the British imperialists to maintain a hold in North America would now provide a pool of low-cost labour and a market for English-Canadian industry. Industrialization strengthened the dominant position of the English over the French community (Ryerson 1968, p. 39; Hughes 1943).

The French-English Fact

In general, all parties in French Canada were wary of Confederation. The final agreement was a curious compromise or accommodation among the several conflicting interests. French and English could put quite different interpretations on the Act. First, the B.N.A. Act may be interpreted as

> simply a statute of the British Parliament, distributing powers afresh among Canadian governments through the exercise of an ancient imperial sovereignty.
>
> (Scott 1960, p. 84)

This was seldom, if ever, accepted by French Canada nor did it gain much support from other provinces.

The significant split was between what F.R. Scott has called the "dual state" theory and the "compact" theory (Scott 1960, p. 87). In this context, the Act was a treaty between several powers. However, English Canada has generally seen it as a compact between several provinces, Quebec being one among equals, whereas French Canada has seen it as a compact between two nations, French and English Canada.

French Canadians tended to feel the Act was a threat to their autonomy. For one thing, the inclusion of new provinces reduced their original numerical majority to only one-third of the total population. The prospect of assimilation once again loomed large and French Canadians felt their language and culture were endangered.

The extent to which French has been maintained as a language is a commonly accepted index of the viability of French Canada at any given time. Although it is difficult to define this index using available census data on ethnic origin, mother tongue, official language, and language spoken, there is a clear trend toward a diminution of French outside Quebec and a perceived danger to the language within Quebec itself (Maheu 1970; Joy 1972; Ares 1963; Vallée and de Vries 1973). One reason for this is that, with few exceptions, the British North America Act did not treat Quebec any differently from the other provinces (Scott 1960, p. 82). The fears of the French Canadians during and following the adoption of the Act were well grounded. The feeling that they were in a minority position was perhaps more prevalent following Confederation than it had been at any previous time. Technically, the Province of Quebec, not the French Canadian nation, was the unit entering Confederation. Moreover, French Canadians outside Quebec were now members of a minority group rather than the Francophone citizens of a union between two nations.

Only one section of the Act referred specifically to language. Section 133 provided that either French or English may be used in the proceedings of the Parliament of Canada and the Legislature of Quebec; that both languages were to be used in the records and acts of both Assemblies; and that either may be used in all the courts of Quebec and in any courts established elsewhere by federal authority. Thus, a minimal protection for the French language was provided. As far as Quebec was concerned, given that the province was and is predominately French, the emphasis was on the protection of English. The English minority gained language rights in Quebec, but French minorities in the remaining provinces were left without similar rights.

In addition, Anglo-American capital dictated that the language of commerce and work in Quebec would be English. The remaining provinces ignored and at times legislated against "acquired" French-language rights. Migration to Canada increased the proportion of Anglophones in the population as immigrants generally adopted English rather than French as a second language. Discounting migration from the United Kingdom, the proportion of non-French, non-British in the population of Canada in 1921 was 16.7 percent, in 1941, 20.0 percent and in 1971, 26.7 percent. This fact is especially significant in Quebec where immigrants have generally sent their children to English-language schools.

Combined with a decreasing French-Canadian birth rate, the end result is creeping assimilation. Outside Quebec, only the efforts at the local level to support French-Canadian activities and organizations, and within Quebec recent attempts by the Government of Quebec to define the position of the province in terms of the "dual nation" theory of Confederation have slowed down the process of assimilation. Needless to say, the strength of the separatist movement in Quebec has stimulated the latter.

The French-English Fact: Equality or Inequality

The history of French-English relations since 1760 shows how long the inequality between French and English has existed. Francophones have consistently been in a subordinate position vis-à-vis Anglophones. The initial "compact" between the British ruling class and the remnant of the French elite evolved into an alliance between Anglo-American capital and the French-Canadian bourgeoisie. These alliances were always at the expense of the mass of the Francophone population which formed a readily available source of low-cost labour.

The relationship between ethnic origin, language and social class, using any number of standard indices such as income, occupation, education or position in the work force, is too well documented to require further elaboration (Porter 1965; Hughes 1943; Blishen 1970; Royal Commission 1969). French Canadians have been consistently overrepresented at the lower levels of both income, and prestige. At the same time, it must be realized that both Francophones and Anglophones are included in the entire spectrum, though the proportion of Francophones decreases as one goes up the scale. The relationship between S.E.S. and language has changed since 1976, especially in Quebec, as a consequence of social policies directed to that end.

When members of ethnic, national, religious or linguistic categories of the same class face each other in a subordinate-superordinate relationship, the operative factor is status. Likewise, when members of such categories from different classes interact, status is compounded with class. It is in this sense that French and English may be referred to as status groups. To be sure, the history of the relationships clearly demonstrates the underlying class dimensions, but subjectively people react to the linguistic or national categories in terms of prestige or social honour (Weber 1953, pp. 69-72). The conflict between Francophones and Anglophones in Tecumseh is a status conflict insofar as people interact in terms of religious and linguistic categories as well as social class. It is primarily the status dimension that will occupy our attention.

It is in this sense that language is a status symbol. Language in French-English relations takes the place of colour in race relations. It is the one overt symbol that serves to set one group off from the other.[3] Any formal recognition of French as a language of communication in government, education, commerce, or religion symbolizes an increase in the status of French in relation to English. Thus the negative reaction of Anglophones to the federal government's Official Languages Act (1968-69) which was written to extend the use of French in the public service throughout Canada may be interpreted as a reaction to a perceived status threat. The Anglophone reactions to Quebec's Bills 22 and 101 can be interpreted in the same manner.

From a Francophone point of view, French, or the loss of it, is a symbol of assimilation. To maintain the language is to maintain one's identity as a French Canadian; to lose it is to merge with the Anglo-Canadian culture. Herein lies a paradox and the source of the ambivalence of Francophones, especially those outside of Quebec, toward their language. It is at once a symbol of identity and of minority status. This paradox between pride in one's group, the need for a positive definition of self, and minority status elicits two responses from Francophone leaders and associations. Firstly, there is the internal response in the form of constant admonitions within the group to preserve, improve and defend the language. Secondly, there is the external response which takes the form of continual efforts outside Quebec to extend the formal recognition of French in the institutional life of Canada, and inside Quebec to arrive at a language policy which gives priority status to French. Success or near success in any of these endeavours has generally produced opposing Anglophone associations. The appearance of the Canada Party in the fall of 1973 was primarily a reaction to the Official Languages Act. Undoubtedly, Quebec's Bills 22 and 101 will also produce opposing Anglophone-based associations. This study revolves

---

3. The fact that few English-speakers speak French accentuates the value of language as a symbol of identification. For Canada as a whole in 1971, 7.6 percent of those of English mother tongue were bilingual compared to 33.1 percent for those of French mother tongue (Vallée and de Vries 1973, p.40).

around the two basic issues of the status of French as a language and consequently the status of Francophones themselves.

French Canada: Ethnic Group or Not

I have studiously avoided, wherever possible, using the term, "ethnic group" to refer to French Canadians. Thirty-five years ago Professor Hughes stated that the term

> is likely to be taken up by a larger public, and consequently likely to take on color that will compel the sociologist to get a new one.
> (Hughes and Hughes 1952, p.155)

This prediction has come true and, in the context of French-English relations, the term "ethnic group" has acquired a pejorative meaning.

Anglophones tend to use the term to refer to all groups of people other than their own. This includes French Canadians, but is more frequently applied to those Francophones living outside Quebec. To classify French Canadians along with members of immigrant groups (apart from the English, Scots, and non-Catholic Irish) clouds the important distinction between the two types of contact situations discussed above and reinforces the ideology of those who conceive of multiculturalism and assimilation as a means of preserving Anglo-dominance.

The Franco-Ontarian attitude is illustrated by an incident that occurred during my fieldwork in Tecumseh and region. I asked an officer of the regional office of the Association canadienne-française d'éducation d'Ontario why their association did not participate in the Windsor area Freedom Festival, an annual event sponsored in part by the Canadian Citizenship Council. She replied that:

> Those organizations always invite us to take part in their programs, but as *another ethnic group* — as immigrants — as a curiosity. This is ridiculous! We are not new Canadians, immigrants or for-

eigners. We were asked to have a float in the Freedom Festival. We refused. Then, of course, people accuse us of keeping to ourselves. But what can you do? The English take part in these things only to help the immigrants assimilate.

From a scientific point of view, it would be quite permissible, perhaps desirable, to use the term "ethnic group" to include both Francophones and Anglophones. But to do so would run the risk of slipping into the more popular pejorative use of the term. This would deny the reality of national conflict and conquest, and cast French-English relations into the same framework as Chinese-Canadian, Italian-Canadian, or Ukrainian-Canadian relations.

Table 3

Percentage Distribution of Those of "French Origin," "French Mother Tongue," and "French Spoken at Home," by Province, 1971 and 1981

	French Origin[a]		Mother Tongue French[b]		French Spoken at Home[c]	
Region	1971	1981	1971	1981	1971	1981
Newfoundland	0.3	0.2	0.1	.04	.04	.02
Maritime Provinces	5.4	5.2	4.5	4.4	4.2	4.1
Quebec	77.0	79.3	84.0	85.0	87.8	88.8
Ontario	11.9	10.1	8.3	7.5	6.4	5.6
Prairie Provinces	3.8	3.6	2.4	2.2	1.4	1.2
British Columbia	1.6	1.4	0.7	0.7	0.2	0.25
Yukon and N.W.T.	.06	.04	.03	.03	.01	.01

[a]1971 Census of Canada, Bulletin 1.3-2, Table 2.
[b]1971 Census of Canada, Bulletin 1.3-4, Table 18.
[c]1971 Census of Canada, Bulletin 1.3-5, Table 26.
  1981 Census of Canada, 95-945.

Table 4
Percentage Distribution of Those of "French Origin" "French Mother Tongue," and "French Spoken at Home," by Selected Regions in Ontario, 1971 and 1981

Selected Regions	French Origin[a]		Mother Tongue French[b]		French Spoken at Home[c]	
	1971	1981	1971	1981	1971	1981
Eastern Ontario	29.8	31.1	33.8	38.2	39.8	44.3
Northeastern Ontario	26.5	26.3	33.7	31.8	38.5	36.3
Southwestern Ontario	10.0	8.8	6.5	5.2	4.1	3.2
All other regions	34.1	33.4	26.0	24.7	17.6	16.2

Eastern Ontario: Counties of Dundas, Frontenac, Glengary, Grenville, Lanark, Leeds, Lennox and Addington, Ottawa-Carleton, Prescott, Renfrew, Russell, and Stormont
Northeastern Ontario: Counties of Algoma, Cochrane, Nipissing, Sudbury, and Temiskaming.
Southwestern Ontario: Counties of Essex and Kent.
[a]1971 Census of Canada, Bulletin 1.3-2, Table 4.
[b]1971 Census of Canada, Bulletin 1.3-4, Table 20.
[c]1971 Census of Canada, Bulletin 1.3-5, Table 28.
1981 Census of Canada, 95-988, 99-907

Our interest is not in ethnic groups as an ideal type, but in the concrete patterns of interactions between two collectivities that historically find themselves facing each other and are differentiated by class, status, power, language and, to a lesser extent, religion.

Francophones Outside Quebec

The extent of the distribution of Francophones throughout
Canada is shown in Table 3. Two characteristics are quite apparent. First, Ontario and the Maritime Provinces account for
most Francophones living outside Quebec. Most of those in the
Maritimes are to be found in New Brunswick where close to
200,000 use French most frequently at home. During the
decade of the seventies the use of French increased considerably in New Brunswick due, in part, to the activities of
Acadian associations and the declaration of French and
English as the official languages of the province. Second, only
in Quebec are there more people using French at home or
claiming it as their mother tongue than there are people of
French origin. If this is taken as a rough measure of assimilation, then all areas outside Quebec show some degree of assimilation. As might be expected, the tendency is for assimilation to increase as people move further away from Quebec
(Joy 1972).

The Distribution of Francophones in Ontario

The majority of Franco-Ontarian communities are in the eastern counties, especially along the Ottawa River; in the northeastern counties with Sudbury as the focal point; and in a few
counties around Windsor. Recently, the Francophone population in the Niagara region has shown signs of growth. Table 4
presents these data, showing that the most viable communities
are in the eastern and northeastern parts of the province.

    The Ottawa-Carleton region accounts for the greatest
concentration of Franco-Ontarians with, in 1971, approximately 117,000 of French origin, 98,000 whose mother tongue
is French, and 83,000 who speak French most frequently at
home. However, the counties of Prescott and Russell in the
lower Ottawa Valley have the lowest number of people of
French origin who do not know or use French. In 1981 the
proportion of those using French resident in Eastern Ontario
nevertheless increased significantly reflecting the increased
overall use of the language in the National Capital Region.
These are the regions closest to Quebec. Tecumseh, located in

the county of Essex in the southwestern region, is an outpost of the Francophones in Ontario. It is the furthest away from and the least in contact with its cultural and linguistic source.

The French Minorities and the School Question

It is on the school issue that French-English and Protestant-Catholic relations outside Quebec have focused for the last century. The coincidence of religious and linguistic affiliation, French with Catholic and English with Protestant, added another dimension to the conflicts. Once schools became an issue, French Catholics faced English Protestants with the modifying presence of English Catholics. At times, French and English Catholics struggled with Protestant majorities in defence of Catholic education; at other times, English Catholics and Protestants faced French Catholics in conflicts over the use of French as a language of instruction.

Section 93 of the British North America Act placed education in the hands of the provinces, but made provision for Roman Catholic schools in Ontario and Protestant schools in Quebec. The Act specifically referred to the separate schools of Ontario and the *dissentient* schools of Quebec. It further invested in the federal authority the right to deal with appeals over infringements of these rights (Ollivier 1962, pp. 87-88).

It is upon Sections 93 and 133 that Francophones and Roman Catholics outside Quebec and Anglophones in Quebec base their respective claims about language and religion in the public schools. Two points in Section 93 had special relevance to conflicts over education following Confederation. Firstly, there is no mention of language. There is nothing in the Act which stipulates that French may or must be used as a medium of instruction outside Quebec or that English may or must be used inside Quebec. Secondly, Section 93 emphasizes rights and privileges held by persons *by law at the time of Confederation.* It left open the status of French and Catholic schools established through custom and precedent, as was the case in New Brunswick, and the direction educational changes might take following Confederation. With the significant exception of Quebec, until recently, each province has experi-

31

enced severe conflicts over the role of religion and language in its public schools.[4]

Bilingual and Catholic Schools in Ontario

Ontario school terminology can be confusing to the uninitiated. Roman Catholic elementary schools are public schools in the sense that they receive tax support and are administered by elected school boards. However, the Protestant or non-Catholic secular schools are referred to as *public* schools and Catholic elementary schools as *separate* schools. There is no provision for Catholic education at the senior high school level. Catholic high schools are parochial. Bilingual and French schools may be either public or separate, the latter being the more common. There are exceptions to this scheme, but the general terminology is adopted in this discussion.

French Catholicism predated English Protestantism in the Ontario region by at least 150 years. The district in which Tecumseh is located was settled in 1701, the oldest European settlement in what is now Ontario. It was not until after the American Revolution that Anglophone Protestants emigrated to Ontario. It should, therefore, come as no surprise that the first schools, primitive though they may have been, in what is now Anglophone Ontario were French Catholic in origin, structure and content.

Though Roman Catholic schools predated other systems in Ontario, of more importance to their current status as publically supported institutions was the presence of a Protestant minority in Lower Canada. The "minority rights" of one group were negotiated for the "minority rights" of the other. In 1863, the Union Government passed the Scott Act providing the legal basis upon which Ontario Catholic schools were to rest after Confederation. Unfortunately for those

---

4. Conflicts over language rights have again entered into public life in Quebec as the province has attempted to redefine its role in Confederation and the role of the French language in its institutions. Within the educational system, the issue revolves around the right of parents to select the language of instruction (French or English) for their children. The reference here is to Bills 22 and 101.

wanting a Catholic education, this Act was considered final and became embodied in the British North America Act as a right held by law at the time of Confederation. There was no provision made for the allocation of other than property taxes for the support of these schools and no provision for extending them to the secondary level. Catholics were, therefore, placed in a position from which they had to negotiate further concessions after Confederation, without the support of the Protestants in the Ontario Legislature.

Though the first schools in Ontario were both French and Catholic, French schools per se, that is schools in which French was the language of instruction, had no basis in law until 1968. Until that date, they were referred to in Department of Education documents simply as "schools attended by French-speaking pupils" (Ontario, Department of Education 1961, p. 2).

Before 1968, demographic factors alone decided whether schools, such as those in the counties of Essex, Kent, Russell, and Prescott, either Catholic or non-Catholic, would be French (Brault 1966, p. 9). The fact is, therefore, that French schools, although with no basis in law, are not without a firm grounding in the tradition of the educational system of Ontario. The French schools did not, however, become an issue until the 1880's. Demographic changes in the Francophone counties were one factor which started the conflict. A significantly large Irish Catholic population entered Canada during the second half of the nineteenth century and these new arrivals, being Catholic, often found themselves combined with French Catholics in French and bilingual schools. The English Protestant population was also rapidly increasing and they, too, often found themselves combined with Francophones in traditionally French-language public schools. Demands for more English and the elimination of French was inevitable in these school districts.

National events were to add to the intensity of these conflicts. French Canada was attempting to establish itself within the new Confederation. British imperialism was at its height. The Riel Rebellions in the West carried heavy overtones of French-English and Protestant-Catholic conflict. In 1890, Manitoba abolished the official use of French in its dual-denominational school system. In 1892, French was removed as an official language in the Council of the Northwest Territories. At the turn of the century, Canada was preparing to take part in the events leading to the Boer War, a war of little interest to French Canada, but of sufficient interest to English Canada to raise the level of patriotism to a high point.

In addition, new concepts of education were beginning to take shape. The notion of a universal public education system was receiving considerable support. Many were beginning to define education as a right rather than a privilege. For the first time, the general public, both Francophone and Anglophone, were becoming concerned with the efficiency and adequacy of their schools.

These three factors — demographic changes, increasing support of British causes, and new concepts in education — combined to increase the visibility of the French schools in Ontario. Ironically, the requests of French parents for additional support for their schools and for more adequate provisions for teacher training highlighted the existence of these schools and thus increased opposition to them. In 1885, the Department of Education issued instructions to its teachers that English should be taught in all schools (Sissons 1917, p. 35). This did not proscribe French, but introduced English into what had been almost exclusively French schools. The French schools became bilingual schools.

Thus began a series of actions and reactions, of measures and counter-measures between the Government of Ontario and the Franco-Ontarians which culminated in *Instructions 17* (Ontario, Department of Education 1913). This set of instructions, known as Regulation 17, severely limited the use of French in the bilingual schools. Regulation 17 remained in force until 1927 when a new agreement was reached under which French schools operated until 1968.

During the period immediately prior to and following the issuing of Regulation 17, the three linguistic-religious groups which became of paramount importance in French-English relations in Ontario emerged with some clarity. Before language became an issue, English and French-speaking Catholics had cooperated in their quest for a more comprehensive Catholic school system. In 1889, the *Catholic Record* of London, Ontario, charged that

> the reason for the attention to the Ontario French schools on the part of Ontario newspapers was anti-Catholicism,..."it is hatred of Catholics... which is at the bottom of the anti-French howl now."
>
> (Walker 1964, p. 230)

But difficulties between the two groups of Catholics had already started to become apparent in Ottawa where the two shared a school system (Walker 1964, p.231). By the time Regulation 17 and its implications were realized, English-speaking Catholics found themselves in a peculiar position. To give their support to English-speaking Protestants on the language issue would remove Catholic schools per se from the centre of the dispute; to support their Francophone co-religionists would perhaps end in the destruction of the Church's hard won position. Language won out over religion and they chose the former course (Walker 1964, p. 242).

The initial expectations of Quebec leaders concerning Confederation seemed to have been fulfilled. In Ontario, as in the other provinces, French Canadians were slipping into a minority position similar to that of recently arrived immigrants. They had become "foreigners in their own land." Nevertheless, the French minority in Ontario was not completely powerless. It did succeed in maintaining itself, in spite of the fact that its future was and still is doubtful.

The Conflict Parties

Earlier I noted that in order for conflict at the intergroup level to take place, social units approximating fully developed collectivities are necessary. Social categories, as defined, meet the minimum requirements. As we have seen, French-English relations are deeply embedded in Canadian history. Our review of this history was at the broad level of national and regional interaction. However, the major object of this study is the way in which French-English relations are manifested at the local community level. We might expect that wherever significant numbers of each linguistic category appear together, language will be one of the main axes around which people form social categories. Further, the significance of religious affiliation in French-English relations, especially outside Quebec, suggests that it too will be an important axis.

Our analysis of Tecumseh will, therefore, begin with the assumption that significant aspects of the life of its residents revolve around these two axes generating three social categories: French Catholics, English Catholics, and English Protestants. These are the conflict parties. This assumption, however, will not be left untested. In the course of describing the community, I will attempt to demonstrate that these categories have meaning and consequences in and for the lives of the citizens of Tecumseh.

Chapter Three

Tecumseh: The Town
and its People

La ville la plus recevante. To those familiar with southwestern Ontario, a bilingual welcoming sign may well appear out of place. But then, upon entering the town, a visitor would be impressed first by the towering spire of an obviously Roman Catholic church. The church and its subsidiary buildings dominate the centre of the town, a rare occurrence in Protestant Ontario. Indeed, the sight may remind one of the towns and villages of rural Quebec. Having arrived at such a conclusion, a visitor would be somewhat perplexed by an apparent absence of spoken French in and around the town. However, closer observation would begin to confirm the conclusion that Tecumseh was and perhaps still is a French-Canadian town. Signs on public and commercial buildings are the first indication: *Caisse Populaire; Imprimerie LaCasse; Ecole St-Antoine; Hôtel de Ville.* A stay of a few hours would reveal that considerable French is used, especially when groups of friends gather.

The centre of town is a little over a mile and a half south of Lake St. Clair. A drive around the immediate area would disclose the remnants of a typical rural village pattern. Apart from the church, the only conspicuous buildings are those of a canning plant. The plant, Tecumseh's only industry of any size, employed, in 1965, approximately 100 members of the town's 1400-member labour force during the winter months, and 500 during the summer and fall months. This part of town is frequently referred to as "the village" in contrast with a more suburban type of development around the lake.

A glance at the accompanying map, Figure 2, will show that the residential area of the town is an inverted "L" in shape. The vertical line of the "L" runs along the lake, with the village located down the horizontal line. Housing spreads out from the church-dominated centre on north-south and east-west avenues. More elaborate housing is mixed with less expensive clapboards, and there are no obviously rich or poor districts. As one heads north toward the lake there is a narrow strip of housing hemmed in on both sides by once cultivated land, now designated for development. Near the lake, housing again spreads out. This is newer and more substantial, giving the impression of a typical metropolitan suburb. Along the lake are larger more stately homes, the back lawns of those on the north side of Riverside Drive leading down to docks and power boats.

The population of the north end of town is predominantly English-speaking, while the south end is predominantly French-speaking. Anglophone and Protestant institutions are located north of the railway; Francophone and Roman Catholic institutions south of the railway. Assessment values and incomes tend to increase as one moves from south to north. Like most towns and cities, the housing and institutions in Tecumseh correspond to certain aspects of social structure; in this case, social class and status.

Beyond these initial observations, just what kind of community is Tecumseh? What kinds of people live there? How firm are the physical and social boundaries that separate Anglophone from Francophone, Catholic from Protestant, and class from class? These are the questions which will be dealt with in this chapter.

Tecumseh: The Town & Its People

Figure 2
The Town of Tecumseh, Ontario, 1972

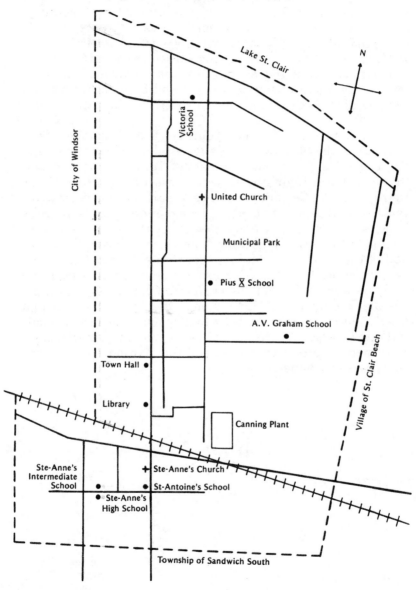

Growth and Development

Although Tecumseh itself was of little if any consequence as a settlement until the early days of the present century, European settlement of the immediate vicinity dates back to the founding of Fort Detroit by the French in 1701 (Chauvin 1946, p. 365). The site was of considerable strategic value because of its command of western and southwestern trade routes. Needless to say, it was coveted by both France and England, but France remained in control of the outpost until 1760.

In the mid-eighteenth century, French settlers from Detroit and the St. Lawrence Valley established homesteads in the area. Many present residents of Tecumseh believe that they can trace their ancestry to these first settlers of the Detroit region. Certainly a glance at early census records reveals several family names still common in Tecumseh today (Lajeunesse 1960, pp. 54-56, 312-334). Others can trace their origins to the heavy migration from Quebec during the latter half of the nineteenth century and to the Francophones who came from northern Ontario in search of industrial jobs, especially between 1920 and 1945 (Blais 1969, p. 9; Joy 1972, pp. 69-72). The history of this region is their history. Although after 1760 the number of both Anglophone and Francophone settlers increased, by the turn of the century most of the major settlements were further west and the lakeshore region was only sparsely populated.

Eastern Approach to Tecumseh, 1973

Early Development: 1800-1900

Between 1838 and 1854 two events occurred which had a direct bearing on the future development of the town of Tecumseh. First, the Tecumseh Road was opened. Running some distance south of the lake, the road opened up the interior of the country and gave access to lands other than the swampy lowlands close to the lake. Second, in 1854, 110 miles of track were laid between Windsor and London. The track crossed the Tecumseh Road in the town just below the present

41

canning plant. Tecumseh thus became a "break of transportation centre" (Harris and Ullman 1951, p. 239). Farmers from the surrounding district brought their produce to the road-railway intersection and a passenger station was built to handle traffic along the lakeshore.

With the establishment of the railway, the village developed rapidly. By the late 1850's it possessed a stockyard, brewery, cheese factory, lumber mill, weighing scale, post office, and four hotels (Paroisse de Ste-Anne 1959, p.28). By 1858 the village was sufficiently prosperous to request that a parish be established there. The community had previously been part of La Paroisse de L'Assomption, and "the nearest church to the west was over twelve miles and to the east about thirty miles." The parish of Ste-Anne was established a little over a century ago and the foundations for the present church were laid in 1871 (Paroisse de Ste-Anne 1959, pp.13-15).

Urbanization and Industrialization : 1900-1974.

At the turn of the century, Tecumseh had a lively, bustling village economy. Transportation was improved and Tecumseh was developing into a fairly significant district service centre. However, industry was rapidly growing in the communities only eight miles to the west and, in 1904, the Ford Motor Company of Canada was established in Windsor. Though the company initially employed only seventeen workers, it heralded the beginning of an industry that was to dominate the entire region (Morrison 1954, pp. 178-180). By 1962, the automotive and related industries accounted for 28 percent of the total value of manufacturing output in the St. Clair region (Essex, Kent, and Lambton Counties) and employed 32 percent of the regions' industrial labour force. Most of these industries were located in the greater Windsor area (Ontario 1965, p. 63). As Tecumseh was so close to Windsor, the steady improvement in transportation facilities meant the town was destined to be drawn into the metropolitan orbit and become a "dormitory community."

In 1921 with a population of just under 1000, the village was incorporated. The new town of Tecumseh was still decidedly Francophone and Roman Catholic. Of its 978 inhabitants in 1921, 86.3 percent were of French origin, and 93.8 percent were Roman Catholic. During the decade between 1921 and 1931, the population doubled. Those of British origin increased in proportion to the total by 8.1 percent, and Protestants by 4.7 percent. Anglophone and Protestant members of the community have increased steadily until, in 1971, those of British origin represented slightly more than a third of the total population, and Protestants a fifth of the total (Census 1971).

Tecumseh suffered the consequences of the Depression as did most other centres in North America. Just before the Depression, an American food-processing corporation opened a canning plant, and in June, 1931, 300 farmers were under contract to the new plant (*La Feuille d'Erable* 1931). Today, this plant is Tecumseh's basic industry; without it, the town could hardly survive as a political entity. Even with this development, the years 1932-34 were severe. The town's administration, along with several others in the county, was put under trusteeship (*La Feuille d'Erable* 1932). The separate school board had difficulty maintaining itself, closing its doors briefly in January, 1936 (Tecumseh Separate School Board 1935 and 1939). Local business also had its problems as the following notice in the local newspaper in December, 1934 shows:

> The little Town of Tecumseh which had suffered in the course of a few years three terrible setbacks in its courageous advance toward steady development — namely the failure of the Home Bank of Canada, the disastrous abortion of an oil refinery on the outskirts of the town and the fatal misadventure of a once thriving brewing plant...
>
> (*La Feuille d'Erable* 1934).

A Southend Street, Tecumseh, 1973

Tecumseh slowly emerged from the Depression, but never regained its place in the economy of the county. Although it still serves the surrounding rural-urban fringe, the advent of more rapid transportation systems, the automobile, new highways, and diesel railroad engines, made redundant a transportation centre only eight miles from the centre of metropolitan Windsor.

By the late fifties, Tecumseh began to share the effects of the prosperity following industrial expansion in Windsor. The demand for industrial and residential land spread eastward along the lakeshore and several new buildings appeared during the sixties. A new municipal building was opened in June, 1961, and a public library three years later. During the past decade, five new schools have been built, a new United Church erected, and residential subdivisions opened in the north end of town. In June, 1965 *The Windsor Star* noted:

> Construction permits issued in Tecumseh during the first five months of this year totaled $179,722.00 — the highest for a first five month period in the town's history.

Figure 3 shows that there is still a considerable amount of undeveloped land within the town limits. Until the early sixties, this land was under cultivation. Most, if not all, is now in the hands of developers awaiting the completion of a municipal sewage system. Within two or three years one can expect the town's population to increase rapidly as these lands are turned to residential use.

One might also expect that this increase in population will greatly affect the already declining French character of the town. Ignoring assimilation for the moment, one may safely predict that the new residents will be mainly Anglophone, thus further increasing their proportion of the total population. Most of the Francophones who do come to Tecumseh migrate from northern Ontario and, to a lesser extent, from Quebec. However, the 1961 Census shows that of those moving into the town between 1956 and 1961, 80.9 percent moved from within the same metropolitan area, suggesting little Francophone migration (Census 1961).

A Northend Street, Tecumseh, 1973

The People of Tecumseh

A wide range of categories are used both in everyday speech and scientific work, to classify the population of a given area or community. Some of the factors to be taken into consideration when selecting what categories are to be used in any study are the particular problem under study, the historical context of the problem, and various positions generated by the issues in dispute. For example, a study of housing in Halifax could hardly neglect race as a relevant category any more than could a study of the centralization of health and welfare services in Montreal neglect language and religion.

In this study, the interest is in the interaction between two categories of people based on language. Given the historical association in Canada between language and religion, religious affiliation is also a relevant category. Social class is also likely to be related to our built-in linguistic duality as well as to religious affiliation. Finally, locality, that is, where one lives in a city or town, is often associated with language, religion and class. Language, religious affiliation, social class and location of residence will, therefore, be the four major categories used in describing the people of Tecumseh. Our ultimate interest is, however, in the extent to which these categories yield viable collectivities.

The Metropolitan Region: A Comparison

A useful first step in describing the people of Tecumseh would be to look at the town in relation to the Windsor metropolitan area. Since Tecumseh was designated as a census tract in the 1961 Census, it was possible to compare the town with other tracts in the area according to certain selected characteristics (Helling and Boyce 1965).[1]

In Table 5 Tecumseh is compared to the metropolitan area according to its three main religious denominations. These three accounted for 94.5 percent of the town's population. Of forty-five metropolitan census tracts, Tecumseh had the highest proportion of Roman Catholics in its population, but had a very low proportion of Anglicans and United Churchpeople.

The same relationship held for those who were of French origin. Table 6 shows that Tecumseh also ranked first among the forty-five census tracts in this category. Though close to one-third of the town's population were of British origin, Tecumseh ranked thirty-ninth out of the forty-five tracts.

Table 7 draws attention to the fact that the average annual wage and salary income per family in Tecumseh was

---

1. Tables 5-7 are based on an analysis of 1961 Census materials in R. Helling and E. Boyer, *A Demographic Survey of Essex County and Metropolitan Windsor* (London, Ont.: The Diocese of London, 1965).

$314.00 below the average for the forty-five tracts in the metropolitan area. Later analysis will suggest that this was a function of the high proportion of Francophones in the population. Nevertheless, the town did rank slightly above the midpoint of all tracts. That is, there were almost as many tracts with lower incomes than Tecumseh as there were with higher incomes.

Tecumseh, then, was about average for income compared to the metropolitan region. What was strikingly different was its religious and ethnic composition. It was more French and more Catholic than any other tract in the Windsor area.

Table 5

Religious Affiliations of Tecumseh Population
and Rank in Relation to Forty-five
Metropolitan Regional Census Tracts, 1961

Religious affiliation	% of Tecumseh population	Metro region rank	Metro regional average[a]
Anglican	6.5	43	15.2%
Roman Catholic	76.7	1	48.3
United Church	11.3	35	15.4

[a] The metropolitan average percentage is not the proportion of any one group in the total metropolitan population, but an average of percentages over the forty-five census tracts.

Figure 3
The Town of Tecumseh, Ontario, 1972
Land Use

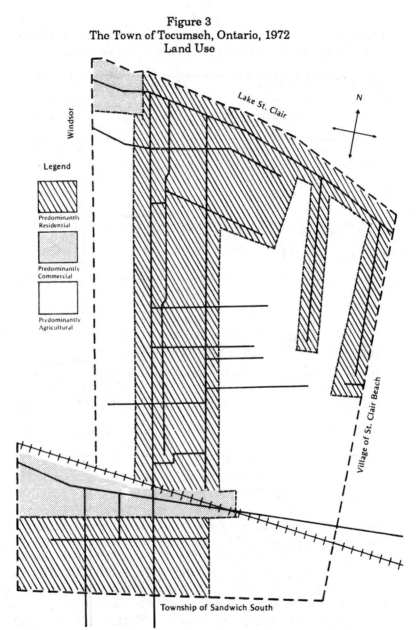

Table 6
Ethnic Origins of Tecumseh Population and Rank in Relation
to Forty-five Metropolitan Regional Census Tracts, 1961

Ethnic Origin	% of total Tecumseh population	Metro region rank	Metro regional average
British	30.3	39	46.6%
French	55.9	1	21.1
German	3.3	41	5.1
Italian	1.6	44	6.0

Table 7
Tecumseh Wage and Salary Income Per Family and Rank in
Relation to Forty-five Metropolitan Census Tracts, 1961

Tecumseh Average	Metropolitan Rank	Metropolitan average
$4,793	19	$5,107

The French-English Fact

The evidence most certainly points to French and English as
relevant categories in Tecumseh. Whether these categories
were the basis for the formation of collectivities or not is a
point for later consideration. However, in 1971 a little less
than half the town's population was of French origin and a little more than a third of British origin. In addition, about
three-quarters of the population was Roman Catholic and a

fifth Protestant. These data were presented in Tables 1 and 2 in Chapter 1. The trend is quite clear. As the population has increased, the proportion of those of French origin and the proportion of Roman Catholics has decreased as the result of continuing pressure from a largely non-French and non-Catholic metropolitan region.

Considerable caution is required using these "ethnic origin" data. In this case, they provide no more information than that one-half of the population possessed male ancestors, several generations removed, who originated in France. It tells us little about the present existence of a Francophone sub-community within the town.

In 1966, a random selection of households was taken from the population and the resulting sample units were classified as belonging to either a French or an English sub-community by a panel of judges who were local residents. From a sample of 167 cases, this procedure yielded the following distribution: 47.3 percent French Catholic; 31.1 percent English Catholic; and 21.6 percent English Protestant. The proportion of Catholics and Protestants is about the same as in the 1961 Census, 78.4 and 21.6 percent respectively. However, the proportion of Francophones was reduced by 8.6 percent.

These data bring us much closer to a conception of the size of the French and English, Catholic and Protestant groups within the town. Moreover, the manner in which citizens have been assigned to these categories is now rooted in observed interaction patterns and the perceptions of fellow citizens. Since our ultimate concern is with social conflict and conflict parties, we might again note the existence of two pairs of potentially opposing categories. There is the French-English linguistic cleavage and the Catholic-Protestant cleavage. The extent to which membership in these categories overlapped, that is, not all Anglophones were Protestant, will have considerable bearing on conflicts over religious and language issues.

Language and Language Use

It should be quite clear that the census category "ethnic origin" does not provide us with any conclusive evidence about language use. An obvious question is to what extent is French used in Tecumseh. This may be approached from two points of view. Firstly, we can examine the distribution of citizens according to "mother tongue" and "language spoken at home." The mother tongue concept, as used in the Census, refers to the language a person first learned in childhood and still understands (Census, Dictionary 1971, p. 26). The language most often spoken at home is self-explanatory (Census, Dictionary 1971, p. 24). Secondly, we can examine the extent to which French was used and the situations in which it was used by referring to our sample of the Tecumseh population.

Since the variable "language spoken at home" was first used in the 1971 Census, I have limited comparative analysis to "mother tongue." Table 8 shows the population of Tecumseh from 1951 to 1981 distributed according to mother tongue. The trend is quite clear — a continuing proportionate and absolute decline of those who report French as their mother tongue. At this point, a crude measure of the extent to which French is retained by those of French origin comes readily to mind. One may calculate an index of language retention by simply taking the proportion of those who report French as their mother tongue to the total reporting French origins (Commission 1967, 1, p. 33). Thus, the language retention index for Tecumseh in 1971 was .56; that is, .56 percent of those of French origin reported French as their mother tongue. By 1981 the retention index had dropped to .44.

Table 9, giving the language retention indices for Tecumseh from 1951 to 1981, shows there has been considerable loss over the last twenty years. Table 10, using both mother tongue and language spoken at home, permits a comparison with Essex and the city of Windsor for 1971 and 1981. As might be expected, though Tecumseh showed significant language loss, a higher proportion retained French than in either Essex County or Windsor on the F.M.T. index. However, by 1981 there is a convergence of all three regions, with Tecumseh falling short on the much more sensitive F.S.H. index. These figures may be compared to eastern Ontario which, in 1971, showed a retention rate of .74 calculated according to mother tongue and .63 calculated according to language spoken at home. Northeastern Ontario indices were .83 and .70 respectively. Selected counties from these latter regions show retention indices calculated according to language spoken at home as high as .99 (Prescott) and .86 (Cochrane).

What is clear from an examination of these data is that the higher the proportion of those of French origin in the total population of a region, the higher the retention index. Tecumseh and Essex County, isolated from the major Francophone regions of Ontario and with decreasing proportions of people of French origin in their populations, do not present an ideal climate for the continuation and development of Francophone communities. Nevertheless, as we shall see, the French communities in the peninsula are very tenacious.

Table 8

Tecumseh Population According to Mother Tongue,
1951-1981

Year	Population	% French	% English	% other
1951	3543	53.5	41.9	4.5
1961	4476	34.9	60.0	5.1
1971	5165	26.2	68.5	5.3
1981	6385	14.9	78.5	6.6

Source: Census of Canada, 1951, Vol.1, 92-725; 1961, Vol. 1, 92-549; 1971, Vol. 1, 95-722, CT-22A, 1981, Vol. 3, 95-945.

The respondents in the 1966 sample were also asked what languages they could speak. The results showed that 53 percent spoke both French and English, 1 percent French only, and 46 percent English only. Table 11 gives a distribution of these data according to membership in the three linguistic-religious groups found in Tecumseh. It should come as no surprise that French Catholics are the bilinguals, with a few English Catholics and a negligible number of English

Protestants speaking both languages. The fact that no French
Catholics speak only English is a function of the method of
classification; knowledge and use of French was one of the
criteria for assignment to this category.

Table 9
Language Retention Indices, Tecumseh, 1951-1981

Year	French Origin	French Mother Tongue	Retention Index
1951	2242	1896	.85
1961	2504	1561	.62
1971	2430	1355	.56
1981	2160	950	.44

Source: Census of Canada, 1971, Bulletins 1.3-4 and 1.3-.2; 1981,Vol.3,
95-945.

Table 10
Language Retention Indices, Essex County,
City of Windsor and Town of Tecumseh, 1971

Region	French Origin	French Mother Tongue (F.M.T.)	Retention Index (F.M.T.)	French Spoken at Home (F.S.H.)	Retention Index (F.H.S.)
Essex County					
1971	58,850	26,155	.44	11,920	.20
1981	47,505	19,625	.41	7,775	.16
City of Windsor					
1971	35,005	14,305	.41	5,915	.17
1981	25,955	10,535	.41	3,745	.14
Town of Tecumseh					
1971	2,430	1,355	.56	660	.27
1981	2,160	950	.44	320	.15

Source: Census of Canada, 1971, Bulletins 1.3-4, 1.3-2, and 1.3-5; 1981, Vol. 3

It is interesting to note that approximately one-fifth of those classified as English Catholics were bilingual. Apart from a few bilingual Anglophones, these would have been people of French origin who were classified on participation criteria as members of the Anglophone group.

A series of questions concerning the situations in which French was used were directed to all those who indicated that they spoke the language. The majority of this group, approximately two-thirds, used French in and around the neighbourhood; 57 percent used the language in the home and in parish activities. A surprisingly high proportion, 40 percent, reported using French at work. To some extent French is used in retail and service activities in Tecumseh, but we can only assume

Community & Conflict

that outside Tecumseh, French, if used at all, was limited to friendship groups within industry. French is definitely not a working language in Essex County.

Table 11
Linguistic-Religious Groups by
Languages Spoken, Tecumseh, 1966

Group	% English only	% French only	% English only	Number of Cases
French Catholic	0	2	98	79
English Catholic	79	0	21	52
English Protestant	97	0	3	36
Total	46	1	53	167

It might be expected that French would be used to a greater extent in the intimacy of the family and its use gradually decrease from home to parish to neighbourhood, with a minimum use in the work situation. That language use did not follow this pattern was partly due to the inclusion of a dozen people classified as English Catholic or Protestant who were bilingual. These would hardly speak French at home, but might well have used the language in other situations when required.

On the other hand, it was observed that people who used French with considerable fluency in neighbourhood settings, such as at social events, in restaurants or taverns, did not use the language at home. In the sample, 13 percent of the

Catholic marriages were linguistically mixed. Therefore, a certain proportion of adults would limit their use of the language to their French-speaking associates and relatives outside of the immediate family.

Also, in a few cases where both husband and wife were classified as French Catholic, they reported that they "felt more comfortable" in English and used that language at home, but on occasion used French with friends. This phenomenon presented a major problem in the bilingual schools. With programs designed for Francophone children, teachers found that many children so classified were no more advanced in French than Anglophone students. Although they were viewed by the community as French, the natural language of these students was, for all practical purposes, English.

The observation that 57 percent of the bilinguals used French in parish activities should give cause for some satisfaction in the Francophone sub-community. One must, however, still account for the 43 percent who did not use the language in these situations. The simple fact that 40 percent of the 131 Catholics in the sample were Anglophone and that English was the dominant language of both the diocese and the province was sufficient reason. The communal life of the parish as a whole, as expressed through such organizations as the Catholic Women's League, the Ushers' Club, the Young Catholic Students, the Young Catholic Workers, and the Catholic Parent-Teacher Association, was English in character. The three exclusively Francophone organizations, La Société St-Jean-Baptiste, L'Association de Parents et d'Instituteurs, and Les dames de Ste-Anne, were small in relation to the former groups and because of their very exclusiveness failed to represent the parish as a whole.

These observations raise the question of the extent to which French was actually used by the bilinguals. The sample data provided a crude index. It was previously noted that respondents were asked whether or not they used French in five different situations. In an attempt to construct an index of the extent to which French was used by the ninety-one bilinguals in the sample, a score of one was assigned for each situation in which an individual spoke the language. These scores were then added, giving each respondent a total representing the extent to which he used French. The distribution of these scores is shown in Table 12.

Table 12
Extent to Which French is Used by Those
Who Speak French, Tecumseh, 1966

# of situations in which French used	# of cases	%
Not used	8	9
Used in one situation	23	26
Used in two situations	19	21
Used in three situations	32	34
Used in four situations	9	10
Used in five situations	0	0
Total	91	100

This index may be used in a number of ways to explore the relationship between the extent to which a person used French and other attributes of that individual. For example, Table 13 shows the relationship between use of the language and age. Though the overall trend pointed to older persons using French more than younger ones, both the younger and older age categories used the language more than the middle-aged. It was this younger group, generally ranging from thirty-five to forty-five, who were participating more and more in Franco-Ontarian associations. These were the people who, in 1966, were active in L'Association de Parents et d'Instituteurs, La Société St-Jean-Baptiste, and an association devoted to obtaining French-language radio in the Windsor area.

Table 13
Age by Extent of Use of French, Tecumseh, 1966

Age in years	French used in 3-4 situations	French used in 0-2 situations	Total
20-39	8	7	15
40-59	12	22	34
60 and over	21	18	39
Total	41	47	88[a]

[a] No answer, 3.

This age group was responding to the Royal Commission on Bilingualism and Biculturalism and to the "quiet revolution" revival in Quebec. They were trying to recreate the French character of Essex County and to provide a French milieu for their children. But the odds against them were great if not insurmountable. The overall English atmosphere of the region, the isolation from French communities in other parts of Ontario and Quebec, and the fact that the use of French was limited to associations, friendship groups, and family worked against the possibility that their children would acquire either appreciation for or fluency in the language. One respondent expressed it this way:

> My children, they don't know any French. Oh my older daughter understands a bit. French, you know, it's good for conversation, but will never get you anywhere.

By 1973 the momentum this group had built up in local associations had run down. New legislation on bilingual schools, French-language radio with a good possibility of television being added, and the adoption of the Royal Commission on Bilingualism and Biculturalism Reports had all been achieved. But the overwhelming presence of English in the region remained; and, for many, French remained a second language if not a mere cultural pursuit. However, new issues could again stimulate the growth of these organizations and, in turn, strengthen the Francophone community in Tecumseh. Early in 1974, such an issue was emerging — the creation of an exclusively French-language school to serve a portion of Essex County.

The discrepancy between census data on the French language and the data obtained from the 1966 sample will by now be obvious. The two sets of data are not comparable since the sample was drawn from the voters' list which had a total of 1,777 cases, while census data was based on the total population of the municipality — 4,476 in 1961 and 5,165 in 1971. Furthermore, the 1966 sample dealt with only adults-heads of household and spouses — excluding all those under twenty years of age, whereas the census includes all age groups.

This issue raises another point of some importance. The major concern of this study is with conflict among social categories or collectivities. Thus, although language was important as a symbol of membership and as a symbol around which issues are created, the focus was not on language per se, but on patterns resulting from interaction among people who *identify* themselves as French or English, Catholic or Protestant. The retention of French, the extent to which it is used and where, are only one set of indices of assimilation. Moreover, language is an attribute of individuals not of groups. I will return to this issue later.

The World of Work

Social class, the position one occupies in the economy is determined, for most people, by the kind of work they do and how much money they earn. Tecumseh is located in one of the most highly industrialized regions in Canada. Manufacturing establishments in the three-county Lake St. Clair region accounted for 17 percent of Ontario's output in transportation equipment, 60 percent in petroleum and coal products, and 19 percent in chemicals and chemical products. Essex County itself accounted for 62 percent of the salaries and wages of the region and 49 percent of the manufacturing output (Ontario 1967, pp. 59, 61).[2]

As was previously noted, automotive and transportation equipment is the major industry in Essex County though most, if not all, of this activity is outside the limits of Tecumseh. In addition to the canning plant, Tecumseh boasts only six small plants with under twenty-five employees each, producing a number of miscellaneous goods such as stone monuments, fishing lures, plastics, pharmaceuticals and printed materials (Greater Windsor 1972). Apart from services to the surrounding communities and its few small industries, the town's economy depends on its residents, the majority of whom, 78 percent of the sample, work in Windsor. Moreover, a third of these are employed in the automotive industry. As might be expected, the majority of salary and wage earners are involved in production and craft occupations related to the automotive and other manufacturing industries. The 1961 Census reported that 33 percent of the town's work force were craftsmen and in the productive process; 22 percent were employed in clerical and sales occupations; and 20 percent in managerial, professional, and technical occupations. This accounted for 78 percent of those holding jobs and living in Tecumseh (Census 1961).

Using the sample, Table 14 indicates the incomes earned through these types of occupations. It will be recalled that the average income in Tecumseh was just slightly below the metropolitan average. What is of considerable significance

2. Measured in terms of value of factory shipments.

here is the distribution of income according to membership in the three linguistic-religious categories. French Catholics reported much lower incomes than either their Anglophone co-religionists or English Protestants. In fact, for each income class, French Catholics were less well-off than English Catholics, who in turn were less well-off than English Protestants.

This analysis can be taken a step further. In 1961, the Dominion Bureau of Statistics revised an occupational class scale developed by Professor Blishen (Blishen 1961). Scores based on an index which combines educational and income levels were assigned to occupational titles. The scores were then grouped into seven occupational status classes. Classes six and seven included professional and managerial occupations; classes three to five, white-collar and skilled occupations; and classes one and two, semi- and unskilled occupations.

Table 14
Linguistic-Religious Groups by
Family Annual Income, Tecumseh, 1966

Groups	Under $5,000	$5000-6999	$7000 over	Total
French Catholic	52	16	10	78
English Catholic	19	20	13	52
English Protestant	8	14	14	36
Total	79	50	37	166[a]

[a] No answer, 1.

Table 15
Linguistic-Religious Groups by
Occupational Status Levels, Tecumseh, 1966

Groups	Status classes 6-7	Status classes 3-5	Status classes 1-2	Total
French Catholic	4	29	11	44
English Catholic	6	24	14	44
English Protestant	13	12	4	29
Total	23	65	29	117[a]

[a] Not working: retired, widowed, or unemployed, 49; no answer, 1.

Assigning these scores to occupations reported for heads of household in the sample resulted in the data presented in Table 15. The relationship found between the linguistic-religious categories and income also held here. Catholics were more represented at the lower occupational status levels than Protestants, and Francophones tended to be more represented at the lower levels than Anglophones. The one exception was that there were a few more English than French Catholics in classes one and two.

Who Lives Where and For How Long?

We have now looked at the citizens of Tecumseh as they are distributed according to language, religion, and social class. Who then was the hypothetical average citizen of Tecumseh in 1971? With respect to gender, about one-fifth of the women in the sample reported either full-time or part-time work. In the main, employment was local. In addition, many women did not report seasonal employment at the Green Giant canning plant, where mothers and older daughters worked during the summer months. Men, for the most part, worked in production jobs in Windsor. Male or female, the "average citizen" was likely to be of French origin and Roman Catholic. He or she may have used French to some extent, but not nearly as much as Franco-Ontarians in the Ottawa Valley or Northern Ontario or, more recently, in the City of Welland. Those who did not fit this profile were likely to be of British origin and Roman Catholic. There was a third type, also of British origin, but Protestant and, if able, pursuing a professional or managerial career in Windsor. Representatives of the first two types, male or female, were usully deeply involved in parish activities.

The third type was more likely to be involved in metropolitan level activities. Tecumseh was, for the most part, only a place of residence. Furthermore, he or she was not likely to have lived in the town as long as others. Consistent with the French and Catholic origins of Tecumseh, 92 percent of French Catholics in the sample had lived in the town for more than ten years, while only 22 percent of English Protestants reported the same length of residence. English Catholics fell between the two categories with 72 percent claiming residence of more than a decade. The issue of length of residence may be carried a step further. French Catholics had not only lived in Tecumseh longer than Anglophone citizens, but 60 percent of their parents had also lived in the town, compared to 35 per cent for English Catholics and 14 percent for English Protestants.

Figure 4
The Town of Tecumseh, Ontario, 1966
Distribution of Ethnic-Religious Groups by Polling Division

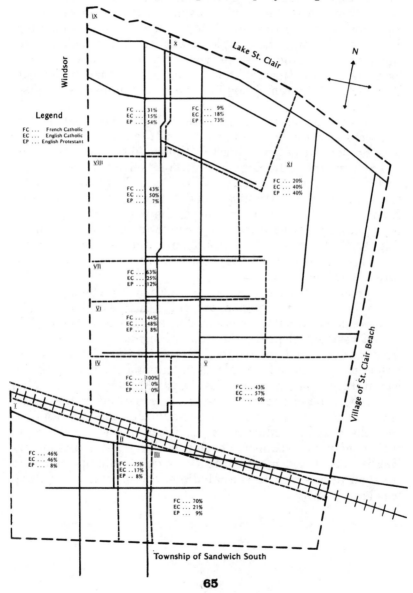

A final question regarding residence concerns the spatial distribution of Tecumseh citizens according to membership in the three categories. Do the members of a category tend to cluster together in neighbourhoods or are they distributed evenly throughout the town? This distribution is presented in Figure 4. Dividing the town into its eleven municipal polling divisions and using the sample, it was found that polling divisions nine through eleven were predominantly English Protestant; two through four were predominantly French Catholic, and the remaining four were predominantly English Catholic.

If the northern boundaries of polling divisions four and five were arbitrarily taken as dividing the town into two sectors, 63 percent of the French Catholics lived below this line and 86 per-cent of the English Protestants lived above the line. There was less segregation between English-speaking Protestants and Catholics than between the former and French Catholics. In other words, the pattern of residential segregation followed linguistic more than religious divisions. English Catholics acted as a connecting link between the other two categories in that they were more evenly distributed throughout the town

Insofar as there was a close relationship among income levels, language and religion, one of the factors contributing to these residential patterns is social class. The assessment values of residential properties tend to increase as one moves from the south end of town to the lake. On the other hand, the observed segregation was also a function of the history of the community. The original residents, French and Catholic, clustered around the railway-road intersection in the south end. It was in this district, polling divisions one through five, that the religious, educational, political, and economic institutions of early Tecumseh developed. Later residents, mostly English-speaking, moved into the available lands near the lake, an area which in the middle of the nineteenth century was largely swamp.

The Forces of Association and Dissociation

We now have a partial picture of Tecumseh. It is incomplete because we have limited our analysis, for the most part, to attributes of individuals — their origins, language, occupations and incomes, religion and place of residence. We may now speak of French Catholics, English Catholics and English Protestants. We know that the members of any one category share certain experiences and hold certain characteristics in common with each other more than with those classified in the other two categories. We know that they tend to live together, come from the same general religious background, hold similar jobs, and share a common language. These combined factors suggest, but only suggest, that any given Tecumseh resident will tend to associate more with those in his or her category than with others. That is, the categories may well be social categories or collectivities. However, we have yet to see evidence of a coincidence of interaction patterns within each category. We have yet to see evidence that the citizens perceived themselves as members of a category. Finally, we have yet to determine the existence of institutional supports. Does the organizational life of Tecumseh bring people together because of certain attributes, thereby discouraging associations based on others? This will be the subject of the next chapter.

Chapter Four

The Town and its Institutions

In communities with two or more social categories based on such dimensions as religion, language, or ethnicity, the extent of social organization within each category may vary from simple interpersonal networks based on friendship and kinship, to complex structures involving one or more spheres of institutional life. Professor Breton has rated ethnic communities in Montreal according to their "degree of institutional completeness" using data on the number of various types of organizations operating within the community (Breton 1964, p. 195).

Theoretically, an institutionally complete ethnic community would be one in which all the needs of its members are met within the boundaries of the community; there would be no requirement to interact with the society at large. Obviously very few, if any, ethnic communities are institutionally complete, but the degree of completeness varies widely within any given multi-ethnic society. If the three social categories in Tecumseh were placed along a continuum ranging from a low to a high level of institutional completeness, they would probably cluster around the mid-point, tending toward the completeness pole. In addition to interpersonal networks based on membership in the categories, the town's religious, educational and organizational life separates people out according to language and religion

In the Montreal study, Professor Breton suggested that:

> the presence of formal organizations in the ethnic community sets out forces that have the effect of keeping the social relations of the immigrants within its boundaries.
>
> (Breton 1964, p. 196)

We might, therefore, refer to those aspects of institutional life that contribute to bringing the townspeople together in spite of their religious and linguistic affiliations as *forces of association*. Those which separate people according to religion and language could be referred to as *forces of dissociation*. Of course, the point from which we view the situation determines which activities contribute to association and which to dissociation. An exclusively Francophone organization, insofar as it brings people together, would contribute to association. However, it is here viewed as having the opposite effect because it would separate some residents of the town from others, Francophones from Anglophones.

Forces of Association and Dissociation

The following is an analysis of the institutional life of Tecumseh according to those aspects that contribute to association and dissociation in the town as a whole. Within this framework, we will look at the world of work, church and parish, the school system, voluntary associations, and the world of politics.

The World of Work

Work links people to economic institutions and in so doing provides the basis on which people are differentiated according to social class. We have already noted that both French and English Catholics in Tecumseh were underrepresented at higher income and status levels, with Francophones showing a greater degree of underrepresentation than Anglophones

This is one of the ways in which economic institutions contribute to dissociation. Income is differentially distributed according to linguistic and religious affiliations. Income levels affect one's access to the market. Consequently, those with lower incomes will tend to live in neighbourhoods where they can meet the housing costs. This, in turn, will contribute to neighbourhood interaction patterns based on membership in one of the three social categories. Furthermore, people who find themselves at the same class and status levels will also tend to share similar values and interests. When this is combined with a common language and religious affiliation, the potential for in-group solidarity is even stronger.

The Town and its Institutions

There is another way in which work contributes to dissociation. Using the 1966 sample, 28 percent of Tecumseh's French Catholics and 30 percent of its English Catholics worked within the town's boundaries. This stands in contrast with English Protestants; only 3 percent worked in town, the rest in Windsor. Thus, many Francophone and Anglophone Catholics not only shared similar class and status positions, but they also worked in their community of residence. It is true that local professionals and merchants were included among those working in Tecumseh. Nevertheless, the situation contributed to a greater coincidence of linguistic, religious and community identity. English Protestants tended to identify more with the larger metropolitan region than with the town of Tecumseh.

At another level, work relationships operated in the opposite direction. The majority of Tecumseh's labour force, 78 percent, were employed outside the town in the larger metropolitan region, and most of these in the automotive industry. At this level, the Francophone worker was a member of a very small minority participating in the larger society. As a worker he or she had few, if any, interests which differed from those of Anglophone workers or those of Windsor's sizable population of Italian origin. If he or she was a union member, and he/she most likely was, the unions were decidedly Anglophone, aggregating those interests which superceded linguistic and religious affiliation. In this way, the world of work acted as a force of association, the major link between the local Francophone community and the larger society.

Ste-Anne's Parish Church, 1973

Church and Parish

Of those interviewed in the 1966 sample, 89 percent indicated
membership in one of the four churches in the Tecumseh region. Two were Roman Catholic and two Protestant. Of the
remaining 11 percent, half belonged to churches in Windsor
and half indicated no church affiliation. The districts which
the four churches served did not coincide with town boundaries. A Roman Catholic and an Anglican church were in the
neighbouring town of St. Clair Beach. The parish of the former

included a narrow strip in the north end of Tecumseh, bounded on the south by an east-west line running through the town just above the municipal park (see Figure 2). Ste-Anne's parish included all Tecumseh south of this line and a fairly extensive farming area to the south and southwest of the town.

Ste-Anne's and the Tecumseh United Church were the only churches in Tecumseh itself. They provided the focus for the Catholic and Protestant sub-communities. The original United Church was a small asphalt-tile-covered building with a seating capacity of about one hundred. A new and larger building was erected recently, reflecting the growing Protestant population in the town. The congregation was established in 1946 as the town's Protestant population began slowly to increase. The Anglicans had initially held services in Victoria School. The present Anglican church building in St. Clair Beach is but twenty years old.

In contrast with the newness of the Protestant churches, Ste-Anne's parish has over a century of history behind it. The current church, a substantial stone building supporting a bell tower visible for miles, is itself three-quarters of a century old. Within the parish, church life was tightly interwoven with the life of the town as a whole. Physically, the church buildings dominate the landscape. It was not unusual for the curé to be present at the opening of new business ventures in town. Nor was it unusual to see the curé or his assistants on hand during municipal elections and other general community events, the Protestant clergy being conspicuous by their absence. Indeed, participation in community life was encouraged by the clergy of Ste-Anne's, as the following comment from an ex-member of the town council shows:

> That's why I went into politics — a lot of us felt from our discussions in the Catholic Family Movement that we should get involved and make a contribution as Christians....the ex-School Board Chairman and the co-editors of the local newspaper, and a lot of others; we were all in the group together. We've always had one priest who was a good social-action man.

73

Tecumseh United Church, 1973

For many Catholics, town and parish coincided. Psychologically, they formed one unit, one identity. For Protestants, church and town tended to be viewed as independent entities. Indeed, the village "is French"; it is part of "they" not "we." From the perspective of the town as community, religious life contributed to dissociation insofar as it separated Catholic from Protestant. It also acted as a force of association in drawing Francophone and Anglophone Catholics together. Nevertheless, one did not have to probe too deeply to discover the linguistic division within the parish, supported by

74

linguistically exclusive organizations and Masses in both languages.

The adoption of the vernacular Mass by Roman Catholic churches added support to the French-speaking group in the parish. Two of the five Masses celebrated each Sunday were in French. In an attempt to keep both language groups content, the curé had previously balanced one language with the other in church ceremonies. During the Mass, sermons were delivered in both French and English, and the Epistle and Gospel were read alternately in French and English. As might be expected, of those in the 1966 sample who attended Ste-Anne's, the ones who spoke and used French frequently attended the French Masses primarily (see Table 16). Though non-French speakers also attended French Masses from time to time, only 17 percent attended with any regularity.

Table 16
Extent to Which French is Used, by Attendance
at French Mass, Ste-Anne's, Tecumseh, 1966

Extent of Use of French[a]	Numbers attending at French Mass			
	Frequently	Sometimes	Never	Total
High	26	12	3	41
Low	11	25	6	42
Non-French Speakers	5	11	14	30
Total	42	48	23	113[b]

[a]High=French used in 3-4 situations.
 Low=French used in 0-2 situations.
[b]No answer, 3.

The clergy of Ste-Anne's, all three of whom in 1966 were Francophone and bilingual, played a fairly neutral role in the interests of the parish's two linguistic groups. In a sense, they acted as mediators between these frequently conflicting interests. This role is confirmed by the extent of criticism directed toward them from members of both language groups, both of whom felt that the interests of the other were being favoured.

A French-speaking education official felt that Ste-Anne's clergy were not doing enough to encourage the development of the Francophone group in Tecumseh. Several English-speaking ladies of the parish were quite concerned over the curé's assigning English-speaking altar boys to the French Mass. English-speaking parishioners objected to French being used as the lead language on a bilingual sign installed on the church grounds during the summer of 1965. An organization with a relatively lengthy history in the parish was disbanded as a result of a conflict over which language should take priority at meetings. These may appear trivial events, but it is out of events such as these that major issues develop.

Voluntary Associations

Voluntary associations aggregate and articulate the various sentiments and interests of a given population and, as such, they contribute to both association and dissociation. Organizations of this type arise out of the divergent and common sentiments and interests related to the structure of a community rather than themselves "causing" these expressions of structural relationships; they do not cause French-English and Catholic-Protestant differentiation, but support such differences. It is because of this characteristic of voluntary associations that they provide a useful device for the analysis of community social structure. This approach was used by W. Lloyd Warner and his associates in the *Yankee City* series (Warner 1963), and by Everett C. Hughes in *French Canada in Transition* (Hughes 1943). Gerald Gold provides a more recent example in his study of industrial development in St. Pascal, Quebec (Gold 1973).

Figure 5
Linguistic and Religious Composition of Voluntary
Associations in Tecumseh, 1966[a]

Religious Affiliation	Linguistic Affiliation		
	French	English	Mixed
Catholic	[1] La Caisse Populaire La Société St-Jean-Baptiste A.P.I. Les dames de Ste-Anne	[2]	[3] Legion of Mary St. Vincent de Paul Catholic Women's League Scouts and Guides Ushers Club Young Catholic Workers Young Catholic Students C.P.T.A. K. of C. Euchre Club Volunteer Fire Brigade
Protestant	[4]	[5] United Church Women Scouts and Guides	[6]
Mixed	[7]	[8] Victoria School Home and School Association	[9] Baseball Club Canadian Legion Business Men's Association Bowling Cribbage Club

[a] This figure does not include all the associations in Tecumseh. It includes those local associations mentioned by the respondents in the sample, and others with which this researcher was familiar.

Voluntary associations vary according to the emphasis they place on aggregating sentiments, of a religious or moral nature, or specific interests. They may act as instruments by which the special interests of some are set against the special interests of others; or they may be mainly concerned with maintaining collective solidarity (Warner 1963, p. 110). "Most associations [will]...combine these features in varying proportions" (Hughes 1943, p. 122).

Though a few associations in Tecumseh served to draw the total community together, most were built around linguistic and religious interests and sentiments. A picture of the linguistic and religious composition of the major locally based associations is presented in Figure 5. The organizations listed in cell nine are those which bring the townspeople together. These were secular in nature and focused on recreational, patriotic, and economic interests.

The absence of French Protestants in the town accounts for the absence of organizations in cells four, six, and seven. The absence of organizations in cell two reflects an important fact about social life in Tecumseh. There were no exclusively English-speaking Catholic organizations. The religious organizations in cell three, though separating Protestant from Catholic, served to combine French and English-speaking Catholics around common parish sentiments and interests. The observation that English is the predominant language of these total parish organizations points to the dominance of the English-speaking group within the parish and the diocese.

There were two secular organizations in cell three which were Catholic in fact rather than by definition. That is, following Professor Hughes, people do not say, "Let's form a Euchre Club with an exclusive Catholic membership." Rather, "they simply form associations among their fellows who [happen to be]...Catholic" (Hughes 1943, p. 124). It was because of this that the Euchre Club and the Fire Brigade were predominantly Catholic in membership and that the three linguistic-religious social categories were sustained.

In contrast with the linguistically mixed Catholic organizations, those in cell one were exclusively Francophone, functioning to organize some parish members around national sentiments and interests. With the exception of Les dames de Ste-

Anne which was organized around the ceremonies of the church, these organizations aggregated and articulated the special interests of the Franco-Ontarian population in Tecumseh with regional and provincial bodies.

There were few English-speaking Protestant organizations. The United Church Women were Protestant by definition, but English in fact. The Scouts and Guides, though attached to the local United Church, were Protestant and English in fact rather than by definition. The Victoria School Home and School Association, which disbanded early in 1966 due to a lack of interest, was also English in fact. The paucity of English-speaking Protestant organizations was due in part to the fact that the majority of Protestants were relatively new residents compared to the strong village and parish attachments built up by the long-standing Catholic population.

Many of the English-speaking Protestants in the 1966 sample who did indicate organizational memberships were affiliated with professional, fraternal, and service organizations operating at the metropolitan level, for example, The Business and Professional Women's Association, the Canadian Red Cross, University Women's Association, the Canadian Cancer Society, or the Masonic Order. The status level of Tecumseh's English Protestants is reflected here and also in their recreational activities. Only eleven respondents in the sample belonged to a nearby golf club, a sailing club, and the Windsor Curling Club, and all of these were English Protestants.

The Schools: Protectors of the Faith

Separate and Public Schools. Of all the spheres of institutional life in Tecumseh, education perhaps contributes more to dissociation than any other. Before Confederation, Upper Canada had a Ministry of Education, created as part of a movement toward a system of common public schools. Roman Catholics were "given the right to withdraw from the local public school and establish a separate Roman Catholic school" (Walker 1964, p. 2). This system effectively separated Catholic from non-Catholic at the local level, sustaining the boundaries already promoted by parish and congregation. In addition, there is a linguistic division, usually within the separate school system, in communities with a significant number of Francophones.

Tecumseh was no exception to this pattern. The town now possesses three Roman Catholic separate schools and two public schools. In 1966, these schools were operated by two local school boards. Toward the end of the decade consolidation had shifted the responsibility for local schools to the county level. The Roman Catholic Separate School Board of Essex County and the Essex County School Board are now responsible for the separate and public schools in Tecumseh.

Ontario elementary schools go up to and include grade eight; the secondary level begins in the ninth year and runs through to grade thirteen. The jurisdiction of the separate school board stops at grade ten; the public school board is responsible for schools operating grades one through thirteen, including kindergarten. Thus, Catholic students who have completed grade ten may attend either a private Catholic high school operated by the parishes of Tecumseh and St. Clair Beach or attend the regional public secondary school in Belle River, some ten miles to the east.

It is important to keep in mind that the separate schools are not parochial, but public schools supported by local taxes and provincial government grants. The so-called public schools, though not Roman Catholic, are not Protestant in the sense of church affiliation; they are secular. Nevertheless, the public schools are frequently referred to, locally, as the "Protestant schools." Given a public and separate system in a community, Roman Catholic ratepayers may choose to have their taxes and children assigned to either one. The taxes and children of non-Roman Catholic rate-payers automatically go into the public system; there is no choice.

Superficially, both systems appear equal in status, but such was not the case. Let us first examine the situation as it was in 1966. Both systems derived an income from local residential assessment. However, the separate system might receive taxes from commercial assessment only to the extent that it could demonstrate that a proportion of the shareholders were Roman Catholic. Therefore, if 20 percent of the shareholders of a corporation were Roman Catholic, the separate system would receive 20 percent of the assessment. In a corporation of any size, with shares constantly changing hands, it was next to impossible to demonstrate religious affiliation. Consequently, the bulk of the commercial assessment found its way into public school systems.

In Tecumseh, a town with a predominantly Catholic population, a good deal of local commercial assessment went to the separate schools since most small businesses are locally owned. But even in this special case, the public school had a commercial and corporation assessment of $333,220.00. The separate system, which was five times the size, had to work with an assessment of $359,470.00 (The Town of Tecumseh 1966).

The relationship between income and religious affiliation built in a further inequality in residential assessment. Since Catholic families in Tecumseh generally had lower incomes than non-Catholic families, their properties tended to be lower in value, and, accordingly, in assessment. This gave the separate system a lower per pupil assessment to work with. To this could be added the observation that Catholic families tended to have more children. These factors, combined with a lower per pupil commercial and corporation assessment, resulted in an actual total per pupil assessment of approximately $7,200.00 for the public school system and $2,100.00 for the separate system (The Town of Tecumseh 1966).

There were two solutions to this dilemma within the legislative framework in which the separate schools are required to operate. The local separate school board might gain additional funds by applying a higher mill rate to its available assessment. This was done in Tecumseh. In 1966 the separate school board levied a mill rate of 107 on its residential assessment and 118.19 on its commercial assessment. In comparison, the public school board mill rates were 99 and 109.30 respectively (*The Windsor Star* 1966).

A second solution was to press the provincial government into making up the difference on per pupil income through equalization grants. The government's willingness to meet the problem in this manner, basing grants

on the ability of boards to raise money by local
levies... [having] nothing to do with whether the
boards are public or Roman Catholic,
  (*The Toronto Star* 1972)

has helped considerably to close the gap over the last decade.
This solution was attacked by the Ontario Public School
Trustees' Association as favouring Catholic schools. A brief
submitted by this association to the Minister of Education in
1972 claimed that public schools were being short-changed
compared to Catholic schools (*The Globe and Mail*, Toronto,
1972). The fact remains that if public schools are short-
changed on grants, the difference is made up by a more
favourable position on residential and commercial assess-
ments.

For Tecumseh schools, a third solution entered the picture in 1969. In January of that year, twenty-three separate
schools in Essex County were consolidated under the County
Roman Catholic Separate School Board. The one board now
levies taxes throughout the county, thus eliminating some of
the local inequities due to rural and urban differences. By
1973, according to the Superintendent of Education for the
Essex County Roman Catholic Separate School Board, "for all
practical purposes the two systems are now equal."
Nevertheless, the problems of lower commercial assessment
and lower Catholic family income still remain.

To this must be added the fact that separate school
boards cannot operate schools beyond the tenth year. Thus, if
a Catholic community wants to sponsor the final three years of
high school, it must do so under private auspices. In
Tecumseh, the Catholic high school operated by the two
parishes draws its income from student fees and the operating
budgets of the parishes. Some saving is effected by sharing facilities and resources with the intermediate level separate
school operating under the separate school board, though even
in this case, the intermediate school must operate grades nine
and ten under elementary school grants. From a Catholic
point of view, parents are assessed twice for secondary education, through their local taxes and through parish contribu-

tions. Should they choose to send their children to Ste-Anne's High School, they have, in addition, monthly fees to pay.

French and English. Although French and English Catholics found themselves united on issues of separate and public schools, within Tecumseh's separate school system there is also a linguistic division similar to that observed in the parish. Based on accommodations reached between Franco-Ontarians and the provincial government in 1927 and new legislation passed in 1968, the separate schools operate English and French "panels" from kindergarten to grade ten. There are two linguistically based sub-systems within the separate schools; two sets of classrooms, two sets of teachers, and two sets of administrative officials.

The French panel is primarily designed for children with Francophone parents rather than as a device to teach a second language to Anglophone children. There is an interdependence between this system and the Franco-Ontarian community at both the local and provincial levels. The French panels or bilingual schools could not exist without the continual political support of Franco-Ontarians, nor could the Franco-Ontarian community exist without the schools as a recruiting ground for its adult members. It should be added that these schools are a consequence of the history of French-English conflict in Ontario, not of any particular pedagogical theory or technique. They are political creations.

According to one Franco-Ontarian officer in the Department of Education, the ideal organization of a French panel is where:

> French is used exclusively in kindergarten and from grades one to three. In grade three, some oral English is introduced. In grades four and five, instruction continues in French, but English is introduced as a subject, as a second language. At this level, some English is used as a medium of instruction. By grade six, other subjects, such as mathematics, are taught in English. From grades seven to ten, English is gradually increased as the medium of

instruction until both languages are on a fifty-fifty footing.

Local arrangements vary considerably from this idea. With the exception of the Ottawa Valley and northeastern Ontario, most districts fall short of this mark, usually introducing English as a medium of instruction to a far greater degree than suggested from grade three on. Tecumseh schools most certainly fall short of the ideal. A very real problem in southwestern Ontario is that, as was noted in our discussion of language use, many parents of French origin do not use French at home to any great extent. Consequently, for all practical purposes, the first language of many children attending the French panel in Tecumseh is English, not French. Though the politics of the situation require them to be viewed as Francophones, French is often their second, not their first language.

In two of the three separate schools in Tecumseh, Francophone and Anglophone children share the same building with separate bilingual and English classrooms. In St-Antoine's or St. Anthony's School, depending on the language of the speaker, little English is used from kindergarten to grade two in the French panel. English begins as a subject in grade three and its use continues to increase up to grade six. Though 47 percent of the pupils enrolled in St-Antoine's were in the French panel, there was little French heard outside the classroom. In 1966, announcements and notices were in both languages; this practice had ceased by 1973. Ste-Anne's Intermediate School carries grades seven through ten. The two language panels are continued in grades seven and eight. By grade nine, French is taught as a subject, but is not used as a medium of instruction in other subjects. At the secondary level, students can take a few subjects in French if they so desire. The goal for 1974 at the regional school in Belle River is to offer five courses in French.

Parents have a choice whether to enroll their children in the French or English panel. Figure 6 shows that the proportion of French enrolments has decreased, with some fluctuation, over the past seventeen years. In 1955, pupils enrolled in the French panel represented 50.2 percent of the total student body. By 1972, their enrolment had dropped to 27.5 percent. A good deal of this can be explained by the ever-increasing number of Anglophones moving into Tecumseh during this period. The gap between English and French enrolments (Figure 6) has serious consequences for those who want to maintain French schooling. Since the children share the same facilities, as the proportion of pupils enrolled in the English panel increases, pupils and teachers in the French panel are less and less able to maintain a French atmosphere in the school.

On the other hand, if we examine the absolute rather than the proportional enrolment in the French panel, we find that over the seventeen years the average enrolment was approximately 340 pupils, peaking in 1957, 1963, and 1969. Aside from the obvious influence of demographic changes, what factors influenced Francophone parents to enroll their children in one or the other linguistic panel?

School and parish authorities can, and do, on occasion influence enrolment in one or the other direction. In the period between 1957 and 1961, it was reported that some teachers and school administrators were encouraging Francophone parents to enroll their children in the English panel or, at best, they were not discouraging this practice. It was impossible to ascertain the validity of these reports. I have observed the practice, but only in cases where English is the primary language used by the parent. The teacher's reaction to this is to suggest that the child go into the English panel since the French panel is not designed to teach French as a second language.

In the other direction, during the early and mid-sixties, Tecumseh had two inspectors who strongly encouraged enrolment in the French panel. This period was also the era of fairly intense activity on the part of local Francophone associations and the "quiet revolution" in Quebec. These factors may well have influenced parents' enrolment decisions and explain the peak in 1963. The 1969 peak was due to decisions made at the county board level. When consolidation took place, pupils enrolled in the French panel in a school previously outside the jurisdiction of the Tecumseh board were transferred to St-Antoine's, increasing the number of pupils in the French panel there.

The fact remains that some Francophone parents place their children in the French panel and others do not. Those who do not have succumbed to a number of pressures. Some parents believe that the use of two languages in the early years of schooling actually retards the child's development. One parent in discussing this matter was worried that if his child should learn French first, he would be retarded in English, and if he learned English first, he would be retarded in French; "but if he tries both at the same time, this might really slow the kid down." Whether learning two languages in the first few years of school does in fact retard a child is an empirical question. To date, in spite of several studies, the evidence is still inconclusive.

In Tecumseh, part of the belief that a bilingual education retards a child's learning progress is based on the fact that many children in the French panel who are transferred into the English panel before the end of grade eight improved their grades. However, this appeared to be based on factors other than a bilingual education per se. First, as previously noted, some of these children came from homes where French was not used to any extent. Thus, from the child's point of view, French was a second language, although theoretically his mother tongue. Second, as children in the French panel moved beyond grade two, the actual load was heavier than in the English panel. The child was required to follow many subjects in both languages, a task that some children are not capable of performing.

Another factor of some importance, especially in a community where the socio-economic status of Francophones is low, is that the child must eventually earn a living in English. Furthermore, he will eventually have to complete the last three years of his secondary schooling in a setting which is almost totally English. The decision of French Catholic parents in Tecumseh is, therefore, not an easy one to make. They are faced with a multiplicity of factors working against the continuation of French education. Whatever choices the individual parents might make, the schools in Tecumseh combine with church and parish first to separate Protestant from Catholic and then, within Catholic institutions, French from English.

The Town and its Institutions

Government and Politics

Municipal Government. Municipal government is perhaps the one continually operating activity in Tecumseh that is almost totally associational in character. Municipal interests — taxes, roads, industrial development, recreation — are common to all residents regardless of their linguistic-religious affiliations. In its fifty-three years of existence, the town council has involved residents from the three linguistic-religious groups at all levels. Of the twenty-seven men elected to the council at ten-year intervals from 1921 to 1961, and in 1966, twenty were Francophone, seven Anglophone; twenty-three were Catholic and four were Protestant.

The town council functions to aggregate local interests as they pertain to the administration of the municipality. Some of these interests are dispensed with locally, but it is becoming increasingly necessary to refer to extra-local governmental bodies. Accordingly, another function is the articulation of local interests at higher levels of government. There is not only the necessity of dealing with higher levels of government at the county and provincial levels, but many projects of regional interest require cooperation with neighbouring municipalities.

The main issues with which the council was concerned during 1965 and 1966 were: sewage disposal, increasing costs of education, youth and recreation (stimulated by a belief in the presence of a delinquency problem), and the usual ongoing housekeeping activities. In the spring of 1966, the five members of the council were interviewed. Sewage disposal was referred to by all five as the most important issue at that time.

This problem illustrated quite clearly the dilemma of the municipality in relation to higher levels of government and neighbouring municipalities. In order to expand, the town had to have a provincially approved sewage disposal and treatment system, but until it had expanded, Tecumseh could not afford such a system. The only alternative was to cooperate with neighbouring municipalities, but such negotiations take time. In Tecumseh's case it took ten years, and in the meantime the town could not expand or develop appreciably.

In addition to the problems over sewage disposal and dealing with extra-local levels of government, during the sixties the town lost control of its library and welfare services to county government. More and more the institutions that provide the social basis for community at the local level are being eroded in the interests of efficient government. It would be an error to assume that identity and community is simply transferred to another level as people become more globally oriented. It may well be that the erosion of local institutions leaves people unattached, apathetic, and alienated.

In spite of this increasing loss of powers, and perhaps partly because of the resulting necessity to act as an interest group on behalf of the town's residents, municipal government provided a major focus for community identity, an identity apart from linguistic and religious interests. The interest in municipal government in Tecumseh was high, compared to many other municipalities. In 1963, 60 percent of the eligible voters turned out for municipal elections; in 1965, 62.5 percent of those eligible cast votes in the mayoralty election. In 1959, 88.7 percent of eligible voters voted against annexation to Windsor. In this election, there were no significant differences according to language or religion; the town as a unit overwhelmingly opposed annexation.

Municipal government is by no means immune to linguistic and religious interests. Occasionally, but so infrequently that considerable press coverage resulted, these interests entered the administration of town affairs. English was the language of council affairs. Municipal employees were bilingual and used either language with facility in their dealings with the public. It was not unusual, however, for informal chit-chat in the council chambers before or after meetings to take place in French among the French-speaking members. In September, 1960, an English-speaking councillor announced in a council meeting that "I object to a language being spoken that I don't understand" (*The Tribune*, Tecumseh 1960). This incident was sufficient to draw comment from both *The Windsor Star* and *The Tribune* (Tecumseh).

Figure 6
Tecumseh Separate School Enrolment, 1955-1972
Bilingual and English Classes

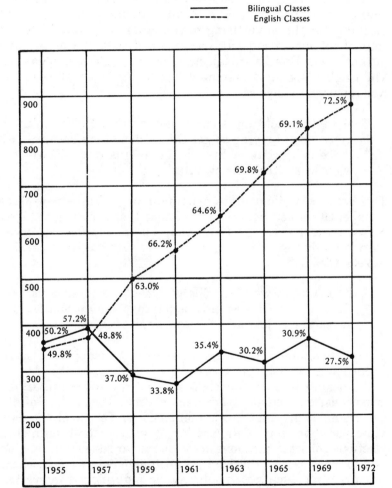

———— Bilingual Classes
-------- English Classes

The same councillor found himself in a public dispute with the French-speaking deputy reeve over the latter's request for a French-language welcome sign on the roads into the town (*The Tribune*, Tecumseh 1962). From time to time, a delegation to the council will phrase its complaint in terms of linguistic interests. A dispute between two of the town's merchants over the fact that the advertising sign of one was blocking out the advertising of the other was brought to the council for mediation. It so happened that one of the disputants was English-speaking, the other French-speaking. The English-speaking merchant, appearing before the council, was reported to have said:

> My father told me some time ago that there isn't much use in trying to get things done here because there is a group of French Canadians who will always look after their own first.

This brought an immediate reaction from an English-speaking member of council who requested that these comments be removed from the record. In another similar incident, a service station proprietor, objecting to his customers receiving parking tickets, stated:

> I don't know what's wrong with the cops these days. Geez, if you got a French name, they're after you for sure. You're just an old Frenchman to them.

These are minor incidents and generally disapproved of by French and English-speakers alike.

In contrast with church, parish, school, and voluntary associations, municipal government is much less a force of dissociation. It provides a common basis for Tecumseh citizens. However, one may well wonder to what extent municipal elections reflected divisions according to language and religion; and to what extent, therefore, council members were potential if not real representatives of linguistic and religious interests.

Tecumseh residents did attribute these interests to candidates and fellow citizens during municipal elections, and candidates and local political pundits also viewed elections in religious and linguistic terms. There was a belief that French-speaking candidates had less of a chance in the north-end than English-speakers, and that Protestants had little chance in south-end polls. During a discussion of municipal politics, a French-speaking resident observed that:

> Now, what's your name — Jackson, eh? Well, if you ran in a local election as an unknown, the people on the other side [the north-end of town] would vote for you.
>
> Because my name is Anglo-Saxon?
>
> Yes, now I know some people over there and they are always complaining about the French clique in town politics.

The following comment, made by an English-speaking Catholic and an ex-member of the town council, agrees with the above statement:

> I've lived here in the village for some time...and I'm active in church affairs so the people over here [the south-end] know me. I got their votes in spite of my name. But I got the votes on the lakeside, too, because of my Anglo-Saxon name. They didn't know me, but they'll vote for an English over a French name. Those people over there are always complaining about the French who run the town. I've told them to run their own candidates if that's the way they feel.

But how does the "other side" of town feel about it? English Protestants have held council positions, but very few since the incorporation of the town in 1921. One of the English Catholic candidates in the 1965 election indicated the north-end residents' view:

> [Upon entering the town hall] on Wednesday night...I bumped into — and — [both active leaders

in the Protestant sub-community]. They said, "Where have you been? We've been looking for you. What are you going to run for?...We need you. We need an English guy to represent our side. We'll put you up for councillor and support you."

In reply to this comment, a French-speaking resident present during the conversation said:

That — told me he was going to support you and — That goddamn — is supporting you guys because you're the only English, I mean non-French, names on the list. He'll support Polacks, Wops, or what-have-you, but not a Frenchman.

In reference to a committee appointed in 1966 to discuss youth and recreation problems, both the Parks and Recreation chairman and the mayor stated that they endeavoured to get all points of view represented. The mayor said:

[The chairman and I] immediately thought of the two churches and the two ends of town in setting up the Youth Committee. [On the other hand], the Planning Board has always been loaded with guys from the Lake. [A past mayor], he polled heavily out there and put them all on. [One of our councillors] pointed that out and said we need somebody from this neck of the woods [the south-end] on the Planning Board.

The chairman of the Parks Board stated:

Areas are taken into consideration; it's the biggest factor. It might be wrong because we don't always get someone who is interested or qualified. It happens like in deciding who I would invite to this discussion on youth....I thought of the two religious groups, someone from the northside of town and someone from this side.

These are the perspectives and actions of those actively involved in local politics. But do the voters behave in a similar manner? An analysis of voting patterns suggests that they do to a certain extent, but not as dramatically as the above data might suggest. Looking at the 1965 municipal election, Table 17 presents the proportion of votes received by three of the five new council members. The Reeve, elected by acclamation, and the mayor, whose opponent was also French Catholic, were omitted. The English Catholic councillor, compared to his French Catholic colleague, polled far more votes in the English sector, the latter receiving about equal support from each area. Similarly, the French Catholic deputy reeve polled heavier in the French sector than he did in the English sector.

Table 17

Distribution of Votes Received by Three Incumbents on the Town Council, December, 1965 According to French and English Residential Sectors

		Percent of Votes Received		
Position	Incumbent	French Sector Polling Div. Received 1-5	English Sector Polling Division 6-11	# of Votes Received
Councillor	English Catholic	26.9	73.1	389
Councillor	French Catholic	50.7	49.3	408
Deputy Reeve	French Catholic	55.1	44.9	514

Although there was a tendency to vote an "ethnic ticket" in the 1965 election, it was considerably weaker in the 1972 election. Once again, the mayoralty candidates were both French Catholics. In the case of the reeve and deputy reeve where linguistic affiliation was split, all four candidates polled about the same proportion from each sector. Three of the five candidates for the two councillor positions were Anglophone, and two of these were elected. In Table 18 the votes of the Francophone and Anglophone candidates are totalled, indicating the proportion of votes polled by each category. The Francophone candidates polled 49.5 percent of their votes in the French sector, compared to the 37.5 percent polled by the Anglophone candidates.

The linguistic and religious divisions were, to some extent, reflected in municipal elections and in the composition of municipal committees. But this does not detract from the associational force of municipal government in Tecumseh. Indeed, it tends to mediate these interests rather than promote them.

Table 18

Percentage Distribution of Voting for Francophone and
Anglophone Candidates for Councillor Positions
by French and English Residential Sectors, Tecumseh, 1972

Class of Candidates	French Sector Polling Divisions 1-5	English Sector Polling Divisions 6-11	Total
Francophone	49.5	50.5	100.00
Anglophone	37.5	62.5	100.00

Provincial Government. Divisive issues are much more likely to be generated in the area of provincial politics. The major issues in Tecumseh around which linguistic and religious interests revolve are related to the school system. Since education

is a provincial prerogative, provincial politics will tend to have
a more dissociative influence than municipal or federal politics.

Victor Lapalme, in his study on the role of Franco-
Ontarians in provincial politics, noted the following three
phases:

> 1. From 1867 to 1937, Franco-Ontarian counties
> voted according to ethnic and religious considera-
> tions, tending to vote *en bloc* for a single party...
> 2. From 1943 to 1948, it appeared that the Franco-
> Ontarian counties were no longer voting *en bloc*, but
> were divided according to socio-economic and eco-
> logical considerations.
> 3. From 1948 to 1967...the counties did not vote en-
> bloc, although in 1951 and 1955 they tended to
> favour the Conservative Party. From 1959, both
> Liberals and Conservatives were elected in these
> counties. The 1967 election confirmed the break in
> Franco-Ontarian bloc voting.
>
> (Lapalme 1968, p. 27)

This was the general pattern, with some variation among the
eastern, northeastern and southern constituencies. From 1943
on, the latter two regions indicated far more support for the
C.C.F. and N.D.P. than was the case in the lower Ottawa
Valley. Nevertheless, given a specific issue, Franco-Ontarians
have shown a tendency to vote in terms of party position on
that issue. Lately, class interests have intersected with linguistic and religious interests, preventing block voting
(Lapalme 1968, p.28).

However, the 1971 provincial election in Ontario did provide such an issue. Beginning early in 1969 and culminating
in 1971, the question of public support of separate or Catholic
schools, especially at the secondary level, was a major election
issue in Essex and other regions with high proportions of
Catholic voters.

In February 1969, the Conservative Government of
Ontario stated that the current policy on separate schools
would continue (*The Windsor Star* 1969). By November of the

same year, the opposition, both Liberal and New Democrat, had declared support for a change in policy favouring the separate school system. The N.D.P. caucus took a much stronger position, leading the debate in the legislature (*The Windsor Star* 1969). Tecumseh voters seem to have acted accordingly.

The town of Tecumseh was located in the Sandwich-Riverside constituency which elected an N.D.P. member to the legislature. Table 19 indicates the percentage distribution of the vote according to party for the French and English sectors of the town. The twelve polls in Tecumseh gave overwhelming support to the N.D.P. candidate, with 50.5 percent of the vote cast in his favour. He polled 56 percent of the vote in the French sector, the other two parties increasing their support in the English sector.

Table 19
1971 General Election, Ontario, Percentage
Distribution of Votes by Party, According to French and
English Residential Sectors, Tecumseh

Residential Sectors	New Democratic	Liberal	Progressive Conservative	Total # of Votes
French Sector Polling Div. 1,2; 8-11B	56	31.8	12.2	1206
English Sector Polling Div. 3-7	44.3	25.5	30.2	1079
Total for Tecumseh Polls	50.5	28.8	20.7	2285

Source: Ontario elections (1969 By-Election, 1971 General Election) Return from the Records, Toronto (Ottawa: Queen's Printer, 1972) p.363.

It should be kept in mind that the proportion of Roman Catholics in Tecumseh, 75 percent in 1971, is exceptionally high, and that they are much more evenly spread throughout the town than are Francophones and Anglophones. Moreover, the issue was not a Francophone issue, but, a Catholic-Protestant issue, involving both French and English. Catholics on one side. In this light, it is interesting to look at the two polling divisions where the Conservative candidate did gain a plurality. In polling division three, he gained 100 of the 212 votes cast, (47.2 percent), and in division four, 119 out of 258, (46.1 percent). Both polls were in the north end of the town, in neighbourhoods which were heavily English Protestant.

Given an issue on the fate of Catholic schools per se, Francophone and Anglophone Catholics in Tecumseh will combine. Had the issue brought the question of French-language education into play, the voting patterns may have been different as French Catholics opposed both English Catholics and Protestants. Though this is a purely speculative comment, the N.D.P. vote may well have resulted from a combination of the school issue and the fact that a high proportion of automotive workers, who in Tecumseh would be mainly Catholic, generally voted for that party.

The parties themselves involved both Francophone and Anglophone, Catholic and Protestant. Indeed, both the Liberal and Conservative candidates in the 1971 election were Catholics. There was no French or English, Catholic or Protestant political party. At this level of political life, the parties contribute to association rather than dissociation.

Federal Government. The crucial question of French and Catholic schools is absent at the federal level. For several reasons, the constituencies in which Tecumseh has been located have traditionally returned Liberal candidates to Ottawa. Nevertheless, in 1965 the issue of bilingualism, the use of French in federal services outside Quebec, and the status of Quebec in Canada were pertinent issues. The following is a brief description of the activities leading up to the federal election of November, 1965.

In the literature distributed by the four parties running candidates locally, language issues were generally avoided by all except the Communist Party. The following statement was made in that party's main piece of campaign literature:

> The crisis of Confederation has arisen because our existing constitution denies French Canada equal status with English Canada...We propose...a new voluntary confederal agreement....that recognizes the *bi-national* character of our country, including the rights of self-determination of each of the *two nations*. (italics added)
> (The Communist Party of Canada 1963)

The New Democratic Party, though avoiding these issues in its campaign literature, made the following statements in a mimeographed copy of their national convention resolutions which were distributed to party members on request:

> We must...clarify and define the special status of Quebec as the guardian of the French language, tradition and culture and guarantee to French-speaking minorities throughout Canada the same constitutional rights as the English-speaking minority of Quebec enjoys. Be it resolved that this convention recommend to the provincial sections of the New Democratic Party that they advocate a *full system of schooling* in the French language where a sufficient number of French-speaking Canadians exist to make this possible. (italics added)
> (The New Democratic Party 1965)

Neither the Progressive Conservative nor the Liberal parties made specific reference to Quebec, French Canada, or the French minorities in their literature. Both made vague references to the problem of Confederation and national unity. A Conservative pamphlet calling for a Confederation conference, referred to "unity through equality," and implied disapproval of the Liberal Government's handling of Quebec:

There shall be no weakening of Confederation. The
dismantling, piece-by-piece, of our country must
stop.
> (Progressive Conservative Party 1965)

In a special election issue of *Liberal Action*, which would have
had a limited circulation among party members, more specific
references were made to Quebec and

the task of nation building, on the basis of a real
partnership between the two major cultural groups
established by Canadian history.
> (*Liberal Action* 1965, p.4.)

All four parties thus adopted a pan-Canadian position on
French-English relations. Within this general ideological orientation, their positions ranged from the Communist acceptance of the binational concept to the Conservative notion of
individual (in contrast with collective) equality. However, policy statements are not as convincing to the voter as the actions
of candidates and their supporters during the campaign. The
Liberal campaign was bilingual in character; the campaigns of
the other three were decidedly unilingual.

French was not used at the nomination meetings of the
Conservative and New Democratic Parties. Both meetings
were held in the predominantly English-speaking section of the
constituency, with about 150 attending the Conservative
meeting and fifty attending the N.D.P. meeting. The N.D.P.
candidate avoided all reference to the issues of Confederation
and national unity. The Conservative candidate referred to his
party's policy regarding a constitutional convention and con-
demned his Liberal opponents for "giving in to Quebec" and
perpetrating discord through their Royal Commission inquiry
into bilingualism and biculturalism. Both candidates concentrated on local issues with federal relevance.

In a later interview, the Conservative candidate was
asked if he planned to take the French-speaking population in
his riding into account. He answered:

No, I don't think we have to. The issues are common
to all — French, English, or Italian...There is no
need to use French, everyone understands English.
I'm after the young people this time. They're not
interested in this French-English question.

In answer to a similar question, the N.D.P. candidate
stated:

I don't speak French. There is nothing I would like
better than to be bilingual. But there is no use trying to fool people. Then there are a lot of other language groups in the riding. We've tried to get a
French or bilingual candidate to run for us, but no
luck yet.

In contrast with the latter two parties, the Liberals held
their nomination meeting in the Ste-Anne's parish hall. Buses
transported people in from the furthest ends of the constituency; a total of some 1500 people attended. The meeting
was conducted in both French and English. French was the
predominant language used in the many informal gatherings
before and after the meeting. The candidate was bilingual and
had held the seat for some thirty years. He polled 63.6 percent
of the votes in the constituency, and 70.9 percent in Tecumseh.
(*The Windsor Star* 1965). In the 1972 federal election,
Tecumseh voters gave 48.1 percent of their vote to the winning
Liberal candidate in an election where the Liberals suffered
considerable losses.

As in provincial politics, the parties were not especially
French or English, Catholic or Protestant in membership. In
addition to this, the crucial issues for Catholics and
Francophones are not mediated at the federal level. Federal
politics tend to be more associative than provincial politics for
Tecumseh residents, but neither bring the people together to
the same extent as in municipal political life.

Association, Dissociation, and Assimilation

The citizen of Tecumseh, whether French or English, Catholic or Protestant will at times come into contact with fellow citizens belonging to the other categories. If one is French, one is more likely to come into contact with English Catholics than English Protestants; if one is English Protestant, one is not likely to have much contact with Francophones. The institutional life of the town both encourages and discourages cross-category contacts.

By definition as well as practice, Catholic is separated from Protestant according to church affiliation and activity. This also removes French Catholics one step from English Protestants. In the parish, Francophones are separated from Anglophones to a certain extent. The school system reinforces this pattern, again separating Catholic from Protestant, and within the Catholic category Francophone from Anglophone. These patterns are further supported by membership in voluntary associations.

The world of work more clearly operates in both directions. People meet and interact at their place of work and in their unions, businessmen's associations, and professional associations without linguistic and religious interests having too strong a pull. However, income and status, being largely dependent on work and the market place, separate people out again as class coincides to some extent with linguistic and religious affiliation.

Political parties at the provincial and federal levels bring people together. But salient issues tend to divide people out again during elections. This tendency was not observed directly at the federal level, but it was operative at the provincial level and to a much less degree at the municipal level. Municipal government, however, was the one activity which strongly contributed to an overall community identity with little or no linguistic and religious interests.

These conclusions strongly point to the presence of social categories based on linguistic and religious affiliations. The institutional supports will tend to promote a higher frequency of interpersonal interaction and provide the social materials for identity based on category membership. Though not yet dealt with directly, we are here looking at assimilation from a different perspective than that measuring language retention and use. Language is an individual attribute, although reinforced and ultimately dependent on a social and cultural basis. In this chapter, we have examined the way in which the lives of people in Tecumseh were organized through institutional activity rather than the frequency with which, or place where, they use a particular language. The evidence suggests a fair degree of separation according to membership in linguistic and religious-based categories.

Chapter Five

The Conflict Parties

Our analysis of Tecumseh began with the assumption that significant aspects of its social life revolved around three categories based on the linguistic and religious affiliations of its citizens. So far, the description of the people of Tecumseh and their institutions has focused on the questions of whether these linguistic and religious categories have meaning for those so classified; and whether people interact with each other and relate to institutions on the basis of the categories. In effect, I have attempted to marshal sufficient evidence to decide whether the linguistic and religious affiliations do or do not yield social categories or collectivities.

Some years ago, Robert K. Merton pointed out that in order to establish the presence of social groups in a given setting, the objective criterion of *observed interaction* and the subjective criterion of *definition of membership* by self and others are necessary (Merton 1957, pp. 284-286). In Tecumseh, as far as observed interaction is concerned, as we have seen, certain activities within the community served to bring people together according to their linguistic and religious affiliations. In other activities these affiliations tended to be ignored and people were grouped according to political, work, or residential affiliations.

The evidence presented in Chapter 4 does not yield precise statements about the relative strength of those activities contributing to dissociation according to language and religion. Nevertheless, the evidence does permit the conclusion that people living in Tecumseh do find themselves from time to time interacting with others according to the language they speak and the religion they profess. Furthermore, the situations in which these interactions occur are not trivial; religion, education, voluntary associations, and politics all play an important part in most residents' lives. It would now be useful to look at interpersonal interactions as opposed to patterns of residential segregation and interaction within an organizational framework.

Interpersonal Networks

With the exception of political and sports events, most social gatherings in Tecumseh were either almost exclusively Catholic or exclusively Protestant. Within the Catholic group one could observe the divisive effects of language as there was a tendency for French-speakers to gravitate toward each other and converse in French. The following is quoted from field notes written after the separate school board nomination meeting in November, 1965:

> Initially, there was considerable milling around, French and English participants, talking to each other in English. Finally, three clusters formed. A little group in one corner at the back of the room...was speaking English. In another corner at the front of the room, a group was also speaking English — McQuaid, Mason, the Carmichaels, and a few others. In the other front corner was a group speaking French — Janisse, Bourdeau, Lacharité, and Durocher. From time to time, people would come in, greet all, and settle in with one or the other now permanent clusters. The " French" cluster did not remain exclusively in French, but switched back and forth according to who joined their group."[1]

This was not an unusual occurrence as most gatherings of any size broke into linguistically separate sub-groups before and after meetings. This same clustering of linguistically separate groups was observed many times in restaurants and taverns, indicating the possibility of linguistically based friendship groups or cliques.

Another indication of the extent to which fraternization occurs across linguistic-religious boundaries is who must be introduced to whom during informal gatherings. Following a session at the town hall just before the 1965 municipal elec-

---

1. Names are ficticious in this and subsequent references from field notes.

tions, a group adjourned to the Tecumseh Tavern. Before the evening had concluded, two north-end English Protestants had joined the group. Both were public school board members and had lived in Tecumseh for some time, but both had to be introduced to most of those gathered around the table, all of whom were prominent in town affairs.

A similar set of circumstances occurred at a house party following the elections:

> The most significant event of the evening was the arrival of the members of the public school board...MacLeod, Smith, MacTavish, Jones, Barker, and Brown. This was indeed the first time that this group, representative of the northside Anglo-Protestants, had socially joined with the "Irish" Catholic clique. All of the former had to be introduced to most of the men and all of the wives of the latter.

Although French and English-speaking Catholics interacted with more frequency than Catholics and Protestants, the following event shows the possibility of linguistically based cliques within the Catholic category. At a small household gathering French and English-speaking couples, all active in parish and town affairs, again required introductions.

> Jean-Pierre Cartier is the mayor and the son of an old, prominent family in town. Bill McQuaid is a councillor; both he and his wife are active in parish and town affairs. The Patricks who have been in town for five years are extremely active in parish affairs. Jean-Pierre and Bill have grown up together (and therefore know each other quite well and see each other frequently)....However, Mrs. Cartier had not been in the McQuaid's house for four years and was anxious to see the renovations. Perhaps they had met from time to time, but the comments seemed to suggest that neither woman had seen the other very often over the last four years.

105

The McQuaids and the Patricks see each other frequently. But the Cartiers had not met the Patricks, they were strangers. Mr. Patrick may have bumped into Jean-Pierre from time to time (according to his own admission), but as couples they were strangers.

To provide further support for these observations, the respondents in the 1966 sample were asked a series of questions about cross-linguistic and religious contact at the interpersonal level. One set of questions asked the respondents about the extent of cross-religious contact in three settings — the neighbourhood, secular organizations, and at work. Using the same procedure followed with the language questions, each person was given a score of one for each setting in which he/she indicated cross-religious contacts. These scores were added, giving each respondent a total representing the extent to which he/she associated with members of the opposite religious category. The results are tabulated in Table 20.

One-fifth of the sample indicated a complete lack of cross-religious contact and 15 percent exhibited a relatively high level of contact. French Catholics had considerably less contact with Protestants than did English Catholics. The higher level of association of Protestants with Catholics as compared to Catholics with Protestants is perhaps a reflection of the residential distribution of each religious category. There were Catholics in all the polling divisions, but several divisions, particularly one through five, contained very few Protestants. Thus, there was a certain proportion of Catholics who had less opportunity to interact with Protestants at the neighbourhood level.

Given the previously noted relationship between language, religious affiliation, and income levels, it might be expected that social class acted as an additional factor in separating the residents of Tecumseh into sub-groups. Such appeared to be the case. As shown in Table 21, the higher the income level, the more cross-religious contact there was.

Table 20
Percentage Distribution of Catholic-Protestant Association
Scores by Linguistic-Religious Categories

	Catholic-Protestant Association Scores			
Categories	0	1-2	3	Total Cases
French Catholic	30.0	60.0	10.0	79
English Catholic	14.0	73.0	14.0	52[a]
English Protestant	6.0	67.0	28.0	36[a]
Total	20.0	65.0	15.0	167

[a] Adds to 101.0 percent due to rounding errors.

Table 21
Percentage Distribution of Catholic-Protestant Association
Scores by Family Income Levels

	Catholic-Protestant Association Scores			
Family Income Levels	0	1-2	3	Total Cases
High (7,000 & over)	11.0	54.0	35.0	37
Medium (5,000-6,999)	10.0	70.0	20.0	50
Low (under 5,000)	29.0	68.0	3.0	79
Total	19.0	66.0	15.0	166[a]

[a] No answer, 1.

Table 22
Percentage Distribution of French-English Association Scores

Linguistic Categories	French-English Association Scores			
	0	1-2	3-4	Total Cases
Francophone	6.0	56.0	39.0	72[a]
Anglophone	17.0	55.0	28.0	85
Total	11.0	55.0	34.0	157[b]

[a] Adds to 101.0 percent due to rounding errors.
[b] Interviewer error, 9; no answers, 1.

The respondents were given another set of questions about cross-linguistic contact. Each respondent was given a score of one for each of the settings (neighbourhood, parish or church, secular organizations, and work) in which he/she indicated cross-linguistic contacts. Comparing Table 22 with Table 20, one can see that there was more contact between French and English-speakers than between Protestants and Catholics. This difference was a reflection of the higher cross-linguistic contact within the Catholic category.

Also, there was a tendency for French-speakers to show a higher degree of association with English-speakers than the reverse. This was due to the religious and linguistic separation of English Protestants from French Catholics, and to the residential distribution of the three groups. English Protestants had far less opportunity to associate with French Catholics than did French with English Catholics. Social class was also operative, as shown in Table 23. As with cross-religious association, there was a greater tendency for fraternization across religious and linguistic boundaries at the higher-income levels.

The observation that there was greater cross-linguistic and religious contact at higher-income levels should not, out of hand, be taken as evidence of a commonly accepted relationship between mobility and assimilation (Tremblay 1954, p. 217; Warner, 1963, p. 361). The focus of this study is not on individual assimilation and mobility, but on the maintenance or collapse of, and the relationships between, collectivities. Data on the former items were, therefore, not considered in the analysis.

Table 23

Percentage Distribution of French-English Association Scores by Family Income Levels

Family Income Levels	French-English Association Scores			
	3-4	1-2	0	Total Cases
High (7,000 & over)	51.0	30.0	19.0	37
Medium (5,000 -6,999)	40.0	54.0	6.0	50
Low (under 5,000)	23.0	67.0	10.0	78
Total	35.0	55.0	11.0	165[a]

[a] Adds to 101.0 percent due to rounding errors; no answers, 2.

However, and of more theoretical importance, contact per se does not imply assimilation. What is important is the nature of contact situations. In the context of French-English relations it was and is the members of the higher social and economic classes who act as the representatives of their respective categories and, of necessity, indicate more cross-category contact. In Tecumseh, those who frequently interacted across these boundaries were the very people who were active in locally and regionally based organizations representing their respective interests.

A final point, our review of the history of the French-English fact demonstrated the interplay between social class and national aspirations. At the local level this led to strengthening the boundary between the two linguistic categories as class, religion and language tended to coincide. The class boundaries are there. The superimposition of language and religion is frequently a result of the activities and interests of the higher income and social classes.

There was, then, sufficient evidence to confirm the statement that interpersonal interaction tended to follow linguistic and religious cleavages, supported by residential segregation and class differences. It would be stretching the point to infer closed groups from these data, but residence, religion, language, and social class did have differential effects on the patterns of interpersonal interaction in Tecumseh.

Religious affiliation appeared to have the most divisive influence, separating Protestant from Catholic, especially French Catholic from English Protestant. The presence of English Catholics reduced the extent of separation along linguistic lines and to a lesser degree along religious lines. Income levels again redistributed the population through sets of common interests and values which criss-crossed linguistic and religious boundaries. At higher income levels there was more association between Catholics and Protestants, and Anglophones and Francophones than at lower income levels. But even here, there was a sufficient residue of people with low association scores to support the presence of social categories based on language and religion.

Discrimination at the Interpersonal Level

Prejudice and discrimination should not be equated. Discrimination is "the differential treatment of individuals considered to belong to a particular social group" (Williams 1947, p. 39). Prejudice refers to "an...attitude (a predisposition to respond to a certain stimulus in a certain way) toward a group of people" (Simpson and Yinger 1953, p. 14). Thus, discrimination is an *act*; prejudice is a *readiness to act* in a certain

110

way toward a particular object. The two do not necessarily correlate (Simpson and Yinger 1953, pp. 19-22). Moreover, one cannot observe prejudice (an attitude) in the same way that one can observe discrimination (a behaviour).

The observed unequal distribution of income, status, and educational resources according to language and religion may be taken as evidence of differential treatment. But our interest here is in interpersonal discrimination. Although some discriminatory acts were observed at this level, the frequency was very low. There was no evidence of such acts based on religious affiliations, but there was some evidence of linguistic discrimination.

In the neighbourhood, at work, and in the parish, French speakers experienced discriminatory behaviour from time to time. One respondent reported the following: "At the shop, some of us will speak French to each other, and the other guys will say, "Why don't you guys speak like Whitemen?" Another respondent related the following incident involving a friend:

> My friend and his wife were walking over to my place, they were speaking French to each other and from a nearby couple, they overheard the man saying: "Why don't these people learn to speak English like the rest of us?" My friend went up to him and said, "Are you talking to me?" The other guy said, "No, to my wife." Then my friend said, "Well, you're talking about me." And they got into a good argument. A lot of our people meet up with these kinds of experiences.

Respondents explained that Francophones in Tecumseh hesitated to use French publicly because they were reluctant to place themselves in such situations. Francophones expect such responses though few could recall such incidents occurring to them. This could mean that because so few were inclined to use French in public, few experienced discriminatory responses. On the other hand, it could mean that the incidence of such responses locally is very low and more imagined than real.

There is another type of contact where Francophones met with responses defined as discriminatory. They were, at times, unable to use French in their contacts with federal employees in the Windsor post office and in various welfare and insurance offices. One respondent referred to:

> a sixty-five year old man who lives on a farm just outside of town. He retired from the C.P.R. on a very low pension. He went over to the Unemployment Insurance Office to see if he could collect. He has had a terrible time with them because his comprehension of English is limited, especially in complex situations like this. I've given him some help. Finally, he contacted our M.P. who gave him the name of a French girl in the office, but no one would make any effort to use French with him before.

Another Tecumseh resident whose English was very limited reported that she had to bring her sister-in-law with her as an interpreter to obtain an unemployment insurance book. On her first attempt, she was unable to find a clerk who would deal with her in French.[2]

Behaviour of this kind was interpreted by Francophones as discriminatory within the terms of the British North America Act and the implied equality of both official languages. In contrast, Anglophones tended to view these acts as anything but discriminatory. By their interpretation, to give special treatment to Francophones was to discriminate against other *foreign-language* groups. "Everyone speaks English here" was the general opinion. From a Francophone point of view, the very designation of his language as foreign is an act of discrimination. Clearly, discrimination is not viewed in an objective way, simply as the presence or absence of differential treatment, but involves feelings about and interpretations of

---

2. These observations were made in 1966. Presumably, the Official Languages Act, passed in 1968-69 will have rectified these kinds of problems in the area of federal government services. The Act was designed to meet these problems, see especially sections 9 and 10 (Official Languages Act 1968-69, c.54, s.1).

the meaning of the behaviour of members of the opposing categories. Indeed, the presence of separate school systems is objectively similar to the one-time "separate but equal" doctrine of American race relations.

Definition of Membership by Self and Others

Apart from the objective criteria of interpersonal interaction patterns and institutional arrangements, there is the question of whether people in Tecumseh behave with a knowledge of who belongs and who does not belong to one or another category. One indication that they did was that conversations frequently contained references to the three categories. A few excerpts from interviews and field notes will serve to illustrate this. The following is from an interview with an active English-speaking member of Ste-Anne's parish:

> Every time something gets going around here, the French want to split and form two organizations. And what happens? Both flop, that's what. That's what happened to the P.T.A. There are two of them now; neither is any good. They always try to force French down your throat.

In a campaign speech during the 1965 municipal elections, an Anglophone candidate made the following comment:

> It's time we stopped thinking about this side of the tracks and that side of the tracks, about this church and that church, about who speaks English and who speaks French.

A Francophone resident attempting to settle a dispute between a French-speaking and an English-speaking citizen was asked by the former: "Yves, why are you against me? We've been friends for a long time. Why go against *your own kind?*"

Imputing differential interests to each of the categories is another indicator of the extent to which membership has meaning. This kind of behaviour was previously discussed in

113

our examination of local and regional politics. Both voter and candidate defined municipal elections in terms of linguistic and religious interests. Appointments were made to municipal boards and committees with the three categories in mind.

The Three Conflict Parties

Having examined all the evidence at our disposal we might now safely conclude that, in Tecumseh, French Catholic, English Catholic, and English Protestant are more than mere aggregates or statistical categories. At a minimum, they meet the criteria layed down for social categories. This is sufficient for our purposes. There was a certain amount of institutional separation; there was residential segregation; interpersonal interaction tended to remain within category boundaries, and the actors imputed meaning to belonging to one or other category.

It is now possible for us to discuss, with more confidence, intergroup or social conflict at the local level. Categories such as these are capable of generating the organizational means necessary for carrying on and mediating conflicts.

The Conditions for Social Conflict

A discussion of the conditions necessary for social conflict to take place easily slips into a discussion of the obvious. But the significance of the obvious may be just as easily missed as the obscure. To miss the obvious — that groups are required, that they must be in contact with each other, and that there must be a certain incompatibility — has often led to erroneous conclusions about social conflict. Errors of this type were discussed earlier: interpersonal conflict is generalized beyond the limits of interpersonal interaction, conflict is posited as opposite to consensus, and is viewed as antithetical to community.

The Conflict Parties

Party Interaction

The presence of social categories or collectivities is one of the conditions. However, the mere presence of such entities does not imply intergroup conflict. There must be some level of interaction among the parties *qua* parties. To this point, Professor Williams noted:

> intergroup or intercategory relations do not consist
> of merely isolated person-to-person relations....In
> addition...there is the interplay of organized interest
> groups...and the representational and negotiating
> relationships of leaders and officials.
> (Williams 1964, p.362)

Interests refer to orientations associated with differential positions in a social structure (Dahrendorf 1959, pp. 174-175; Parsons 1954, p. 330). In the case of minority groups, an unequal distribution of power, wealth, and status provides the positional basis for differentiated orientations of subordinate and superordinate groups.

If incumbents of positions carrying common interests are conscious of these interests, one may refer to *manifest* as opposed to *latent* interests (Dahrendorf 1959, p. 178). Individuals and organized groups emerge from relatively clearly demarcated social categories as promoters of manifest interests. "Manifest interests are the programs of organized groups" (Dahrendorf 1959, p. 178). In the context of conflict systems, I will refer to such organized groups as *conflict agencies*.

Conflict agents serve a similar function, but refer to individuals rather than organized groups. A conflict agent promotes the interests of a social category because of a position held in an institutional framework. For example, a county superintendent of bilingual schools, by virtue of a position in the school system, is *ipso facto* a promoter of the interests of the French Catholic party though s/he may not represent a particular association or conflict agency. The actions of conflict agencies and agents represent the points of contact between the parties. It is through conflict agencies and agents that interaction between the parties takes place.

Conflict Agencies

For our purposes, any voluntary association that is based on language and/or religion is a potential conflict agency. Associations of this type may serve one or more functions within linguistic religious categories. They may exhibit a *supportive* function insofar as they contribute to internal solidarity, an *interest-articulating* function insofar as they place party interests before the public or the opponent, and an *interest-aggregating* function insofar as they gather local party interests together in order to articulate them at a higher level. One or other of the latter two functions must be present if an association is to be designated as a conflict agency.

Through an analysis of the records of local and extra-local associations related to the three Tecumseh parties and observations of the activities of these associations, conflict agencies were identified. Referring to Figure 5, any of the associations appearing in cells one, three, five, or eight were potential conflict agencies. That is, any one may have been involved in aggregating and articulating the special interests of the conflict parties to which they were related.

A step-by-step process of elimination was used to arrive at a final analysis of those associations which could be designated as conflict agencies. Those associations were eliminated where observations of meetings and unstructured interviews of members did not reveal interest-aggregation and articulation functions. A structured interview schedule was then administered to the officers of the remaining associations, probing the activities of each. If these data indicated the presence of the above-mentioned functions, the records (minutes, correspondence, constitutions, etc.,) were analyzed in depth.

The end result was an analysis of the records of the following local associations:

1. The St. Anthony's-Ste-Anne's Catholic Parent-Teacher Association (C.P.T.A.);

2. The Pius X Catholic Parent-Teacher Association (C.P.T.A.);

   3. L'Association de Parents et d'Instituteurs (A.P.I.);

   4. La Société St-Jean-Baptiste (S.S.J.B.).

At the local level, the first two were involved, primarily, in the special interests of the Catholic sub-community as far as education was concerned. The remaining two were involved in the special interests of the French Catholic party. It is of some importance that there were no local English Protestant conflict agencies. The significance of this observation will receive attention later. It is of equal importance that the two parent-teacher associations were involved in Catholic rather than English Catholic interests per se. Certainly, the mixed membership of the P.T.A.'s mitigated a purely linguistic alignment.

L'Association de Parents et d'instituteurs. The constitution of La Fédération des Associations de Parents et d'Instituteurs de langue française d'Ontario contained the following statement on the purposes of locally affiliated associations: "La raison d'être de toute A.P.I. c'est l'education chrétienne de la jeunesse franco-ontarienne" (A.P.I. 1964, p. 2). This general statement was developed further in the constitution, referring to more specific organizational goals. These goals were similar to those of any parent-teacher association, stressing the necessity of cooperation between home and school. The statement of purpose alone did not provide sufficient evidence to conclude that the A.P.I. was a conflict agency.

   Certainly the emphasis on the education of *Franco-Ontarian* children and the fact that the Association was French-speaking gave it a supportive function. And, indeed, an analysis of the minutes of the Tecumseh A.P.I. between January, 1956 and January, 1966 indicated that the supportive function was stressed. Displays and sales of French-language books for children; announcements of where one could buy French books and records, donations of French books to the school library; participation in French-Canadian national holidays; evenings devoted to French-Canadian folk songs; and support given to a bilingual kindergarten were all examples of activities contributing to the solidarity of the ingroup. Programs of this type, along with customary money-raising projects such as bake sales, card parties, or dances, occupied most of the energy of the Association. Money-raising activities were frequently conducted in cooperation with the English-speaking Catholic Parent-Teacher Association.

The response to language issues was also more support-ive than interest-oriented. The phrase, "Le curé nous dit un mot d'encouragement sur la langue française," appeared in the minutes with some regularity. At the October, 1957 meeting, the chairman of the program committee "demande la coopéra-tion des parents pour continuer l'oeuvre que nous avons com-mencé. Parlez français à la maison pour faciliter la tâche des mâitresses." At another meeting the president encouraged the members "... à venir et de jaser en français méme si les membres font des fautes."

In only eight of the sixty-two recorded meetings over the ten year period did any activities occur that could be classified as interest-aggregation and articulation. This involved such activities as discussions on the lack of use of French in the schoolyard; criticism of the teaching of French in grade one in the bilingual school; involvement in requests for French radio and television programs; and requests sent to the municipal library about the purchase and condition of French-language books. Nevertheless, the A.P.I. may be designated as a conflict agency. The requirement for this designation is that the Association exhibit some activities indicating an interest-ag-gregation and articulation function. The extent to which asso-ciations are involved in these kinds of activities refers to the intensity of a conflict situation.

In 1966, the president of the local A.P.I. was aware of the Association's connection with the special interests of the French Catholic party. In answer to a question concerning the goals of the Association, he answered, "Creating better rela-tions between parent-teacher for the child's benefit." In re-sponse to this, he was further asked, "Is this your primary goal?" The reply was, "No, we also represent the bilingual group and through our regional and provincial association, we represent them to the government." Further interviews of people associated with the regional and provincial associations indicated that these latter bodies are far more involved in in-terest-aggregating and articulating functions than the local associations.

The Conflict Parties

Local A.P.I.'s are affiliated with regional boards and the provincially based Federation. The regional board, in the case of Tecumseh, operated out of Windsor on behalf of the associations in the metropolitan area. The regional and provincial organizations aggregated local interests and articulated these at the metropolitan and provincial levels. This involved representation to the provincial legislature and the Department of Education.

La Société St-Jean-Baptiste. The same procedure was followed in analyzing the activities of La Société St-Jean-Baptiste and the two Catholic Parent-Teacher Associations. The stated purpose of the former society placed it in a much broader context within the French-speaking community than the A.P.I.

> La Société St-Jean-Baptiste est la société nationale des Canadiens français. Cet organisme groupe tous les Canadiens de langue et de mentalité françaises de la province, qui veulent se joindre à ses rangs et constituer une société de vigilance constante pour sauvegarde des droits et des intérêts des groupes français de l'Ontario, et travailler à. leur avancement culturel, social et économique. (S.S.J.B., Ontario)

Devoted to French-Canadian nationalism per se, the S.S.J.B. was at once a fraternal, mutual aid and insurance service (through the affiliated Caisse Populaire) and a recreational and political society in contrast with the specifically educational interests of the A.P.I. It was also organized on a parish rather than a school-district basis. The local S.S.J.B. was a parish organization joining other such organizations in regularly scheduled corporate communions.

The president of the local S.S.J.B. viewed its primary objective as being "conserver la langue et la fois." Given these objectives, it might be expected that this society would be more oriented toward interest-aggregation and articulation than the A.P.I. Such was not the case. The analysis of the Society's minutes from January, 1960 to December, 1965 showed a strong emphasis on supportive activities. In only three out of forty-two general meetings was there any evidence of activities indicating interest articulation. Those involved correspondence with the Tecumseh and neighbouring town councils regarding bilingual signs on their buildings; a similar correspondence with the Ontario Liquor Control Board regarding its building in Tecumseh; efforts to have a bilingual notice board in one of the local schools; and other activities similar to those in which the A.P.I. was involved. In many cases, the two associations cooperated in promoting the interests of the local French Catholic party.

As with the A.P.I., it was the regional and provincial organizations of the S.S.J.B. which were oriented toward aggregating and articulating special interests. The Tecumseh Société was affiliated with the L'Association St-Jean-Baptiste de l'Ouest de l'Ontario and the provincial Federation. The goals of the regional association, according to its president, were:

> to preserve the language and our national identity, to keep alive and renew the French-speaking community. Our work is directed toward social events, toward the schools and toward encouraging parents to make sure their children learn French.
>
> Now, for example, you will find in a parish that a curé will not use French — the English would object if he did. We, as a group can ask for French; we represent the French-speaking community.

Following this statement, the respondent was asked, "What about local schools, the bilingual classes? Do you have problems or issues to deal with there?" He replied:

> Yes, but we don't get involved. The provincial body represents us here along with l'Association canadienne-française d'éducation d'Ontario — briefs and letters are sent to the government and the Department of Education.

120

The Conflict Parties

L'Association canadienne-française d'éducation d'Ontario (A.C.F.E.0.) is a major representative of Francophone interests in Ontario.[3] Through their regional and provincial organizations, the Tecumseh A.P.I. and S.S.J.B., were affiliated with this organization. The A.C.F.E.0., whose purpose was "La vigilante protection de tous les intérêts de Canadiens français de l'Ontario et la juste revendication de tous leurs droits" (A.C.F.E.0. 1965, p. 1), aggregated the interests of the total French-speaking community in Ontario and articulated these directly with the centres of decision making.

In addition to the A.P.I., and the S.S.J.B., the A.C.F.E.O. drew into its membership twelve other associations. Many French speaking citizens in Tecumseh were members of these other associations which operated beyond the local level. Included among these were: L'Association des enseignants franco-ontariens (The Franco-Ontarian Teachers' Association), L Association des Commissions des écoles bilingues d'Ontario (The Association of Bilingual School Boards of Ontario), and L'Association des écoles secondaires privées franco-ontariennes (The Association of Franco Ontarian Private Secondary Schools).

The Catholic Parent-Teacher Association. Whereas the A.P.I. involved parents with children enrolled in the French panel, the two local Catholic Parent-Teacher Associations involved parents with children enrolled in the English panel. Since a number of French-speaking parents had children in the English panel, the membership of the C.P.T.A.'s was linguistically mixed. The result of this mixed membership was conflicting linguistic allegiances within the two associations which, in turn, inhibited them from representing English Catholic interests as such. The emphasis was placed on Catholic interests in education. Nevertheless, the existence of a corresponding French-speaking structure implied that the C.P.T.A's represented English-speaking interests. Moreover, the association aggregating local interests and articulating these at the provincial level for English Catholics was called the Ontario *English Catholic* Education Association in contrast

---

3. The name was later changed to L'Association canadienne-française de l'Ontario (A.C.F.O.) indicating a broadening of interests and activities.

with L'Association *canadienne-française* d'Education d'Ontario. Thus, in a town such as Tecumseh, a C.P.T.A. would find itself in a rather ambivalent position. From one point of view, it represented English Catholic interests and yet, because of its mixed membership, it was more inclined to limit its concerns to Catholic interests without any linguistic connotations.

The analysis of the minutes and correspondence of the two C.P.T.A's indicated a primarily supportive function, much more so than their French-speaking counterpart, the A.P.I. This may have been due to the ambivalence resulting from mixed membership — an ambivalence which could partially be solved by avoiding issues that might bring out linguistic interests. The St. Anthony's-Ste-Anne's C.P.T.A., the older of the two groups, involved parents from St. Anthony's School, Ste-Anne's Intermediate School, and Ste-Anne's High School. Pius X's C.P.T.A. was formed in September, 1960 for north-end parents sending their children to the new Pius X School.

The main activities of both associations consisted of various money-raising projects, and a quasi-educational program promoted through speakers, films, discussions, etc. In a separate school system, the importance of auxiliary funds raised by such associations should not be underestimated. With less income per pupil than the public schools, a separate school needs these extra funds for libraries and special equipment. Interest-articulation activity took place through contacts with provincial and regional C.P.T.A. bodies with which the local associations are affiliated. Correspondence from these extra-local organizations called for local discussion on issues presented in the form of resolutions to be handled at province-wide conventions.

The issues were placed in a Catholic versus Protestant, rather than a French versus English, context. The following is an excerpt from a letter from the Federation of Catholic Parent-Teacher Associations of Ontario to local associations:

> As you will recall, an important segment of these resolutions dealt with problems of the Separate Schools and the need for a thorough knowledge and understanding of the school system in the Province,

and in particular of the financial strait jacket in which our schools are placed.

...To insure proper action, one or two meetings in the year should be devoted to this subject. Special speakers, preferably those having a sound knowledge of the school assessment system, should be invited to speak.... (C.P.T.A. 1961)

At a meeting of the St. Anthony's-Ste-Anne's C.P.T.A. in January, 1966, a member of the Federation executive invited to speak referred to the Federation as the "liaison between what the people want and what the government will give us. He went on to say that "it is the Federation that represents Catholic interests in government circles."

At an earlier meeting of the same association, the annual discussion of resolutions for the provincial convention resulted in the following discussion:

President: If there are any resolutions for Federation, we should bring them up now.

Parent: We should send in a resolution asking that the government give Catholic schools grants up to grade thirteen, just like they do to the others.

President: Yes, well, I think the Bishop is working on that.

School Principal: The Bishop is a man of the cloth and as such he doesn't have, the same influence that we have. This is political and we, after all, are the voters. Maybe a resolution isn't strong enough; maybe we should have a petition.

Another Parent: I agree. We've got to do something. I approve of a resolution.

The following resolution was passed:

Moved by — seconded by — , that members of the Tecumseh C.P.T.A. resolve that the government take over the operating cost of Catholic high schools so that all our children have equal financial assistance in education.

A similar resolution was passed by the Pius X's Association a month later.

With a similar structure to its French counterpart, the C.P.T.A. Federation is a member of the English Catholic Education Association of Ontario (E.C.E.A.O.), along with the Ontario Separate School Trustees' Association, the Ontario English Catholic Teachers' Association, and the Association of Catholic High School Boards of Ontario. This association, whose stated purpose was:

> ...to foster, unite, and co-ordinate all efforts to pro-
> vide Catholic education in Ontario....To provide a
> medium which will effectively express and encour-
> age Catholic thought and action on questions affect-
> ing education.... (E.C.E.A.O. 1966).

is the main representative of English Catholic interests in Ontario.

Within the Catholic category in Tecumseh, then, there were four associations which met the criteria for conflict agencies: the A.P.I., and the S.S.J.B., representing French Catholic interests; and the two C.P.T.A.'s directly representing Catholic interests, but indirectly through regional and provincial organizations representing English Catholic interests. All four agencies had emerged from identifiable conflict parties. The special interests of these parties were the programs of their corresponding agencies. The observation that these agencies were mainly supportive at the local level, articulating interests only through regional and provincial bodies, had certain effects on the conflict system at the local level.

One of these effects was the absence of English Protestant conflict agencies in Tecumseh. With interests being articulated by extra-local agencies, there was little to stimulate activity locally. But of greater import was the fact that there were two school systems. Thus, locally, there was no contact over educational issues between English Protestants and French or English Catholics. This separation actually functioned to reduce rather than increase the potential for overt conflict. Even at the provincial level, there were few vocal agencies representing English Protestant interests. The

124

The Conflict Parties

Orange Lodge, which was so actively anti-French and anti-Catholic during the latter part of the nineteenth century and the early part of this century, had almost disappeared from the scene. In 1965, the Protestant League of Ontario received attention from the press when it appeared before the federal government's Royal Commission on Bilingualism and Biculturalism. The spokesman for this association, reminding the Commission that the French Canadians "are a conquered people," suggested that bilingualism will divide rather than unite the country (*Le Droit* 1965).

Apart from the specific characteristics of Tecumseh, there were other factors that can be regarded as responsible for the observed paucity of English Protestant conflict agencies. The English Protestants hold the superordinate position within the French-English and Protestant-Catholic conflict systems. In a superordinate-subordinate relationship, the former party seldom has rights to defend or gain and, unless it perceives a threat to the system, it will tend not to develop special organizations to answer the demands of the latter party. Since the nature of the rights in question places the debate at a governmental level, the government, in fact rather than by intent, becomes the conflict agency for the superordinate party. It becomes a case of French Catholic versus the "English Protestant" government of Ontario and English Catholic versus the "Protestant" government of Ontario. A further check is placed on the development of English Protestant conflict agencies by restricting the dialogue to the offices of the Department of Education. This gives the issues far less visibility than if they were to be debated on the floor of the legislative assembly.

A complex system has developed since the accommodation of 1927 so that French-English and Protestant-Catholic issues pertaining to education tend to be dealt with as administrative rather than as political problems. That is, the issues are articulated in a bureaucratic setting within government departments rather than on the floor of the legislature. Part of this system was revealed in an analysis of conflict *agents* as differentiated from conflict *agencies*.

Conflict Agents

The category of conflict agent refers to status-role complexes within institutional structures which function, either latently or manifestly, to articulate party interests.[4] A conflict agent is not an agency representative, but a position within an institutional structure used by party members and conflict agencies to promote their special interests. The empirical problem was to identify such positions, if any, within the educational, political, and religious institutions of Tecumseh.

The School System. Two schools in Tecumseh operated both French and English panels. As would be expected, students in the French panels were taught by French-speaking Catholics, and in the English panels by English-speaking Catholics. From the schools' point of view, both sets of teachers function to promote identical educational goals, but the fact that the teaching staff was divided along linguistic lines implied there was a potential for articulating linguistic interests. This notion may be further elaborated by using Professor Merton's concepts of status-set and role-set (Merton 1957, pp. 369-370).

The position of bilingual teacher carried the customary elementary school teacher role-set relating the incumbent to colleagues, Board of Education members, school principal, etc. In addition to this, there was also a role-set relating the teacher to the French Catholic party — a role-set involving French-speaking parents, the superintendent of French-language schools, French-speaking members of the Board of Education, and French Catholic conflict agencies. That is, the positions of bilingual and English teacher carried linguistically as well as an educationally based role-sets.

Accompanying the dual role-set, a particular bilingual or English teacher will carry a status-set which may further tie him or her to linguistic interests. A bilingual teacher is generally a Franco-Ontarian and probably a member of the

---

4. R.K. Merton's conceptualization of status-role is used here. Status is viewed as "a position in a social system occupied by designated individuals." Role refers to the behavioural enacting of the patterned expectations attributed to that position (Merton 1957, p.368).

local Association de Parents et d'Instituteurs, La Société St-Jean-Baptiste, L'Association canadienne-française d'éducation d'Ontario, and most certainly a member of l'Association des enseignants franco-ontariens. Likewise, an English teacher will most likely be an English Catholic, a member of the English Catholic Teachers' Association and, indirectly, the English Catholic Education Association of Ontario.

It is in this sense that a given position in an institutional structure functions as a conflict agent. Through the role-sets associated with the bilingual and English teachers and the status-sets which each incumbent generally carries, the interests of the linguistic-religious parties were built into these positions. From the viewpoint of the school system, these were unintended and generally unrecognized consequences. That is, the conflict-agent component is a latent function. To be sure, there were bilingual and English teachers, but the formal distinction is not according to linguistic affiliation. A bilingual teacher is one who holds a French certificate from a recognized training school; one need not be a Franco-Ontarian to obtain such a certificate. Similarly, an English teacher holds an English certificate and need not be English. What occurs in fact, however, is that although some Franco-Ontarians hold English or English and French certificates, few native English-speakers hold French certificates. The training schools granting French certificates are *de facto* Franco-Ontarian institutions. Their graduates have themselves come up through the bilingual elementary school system. From a Franco-Ontarian viewpoint, they are "our teachers."

Conflict agents may thus be located at several levels within the educational system. In each of the two schools, if the principal was English, a French-speaking vice-principal or senior teacher was appointed to supervise and administer the French panel. In 1965, both St. Anthony's and Ste-Anne's had English principals and special appointees to direct the French panels. Both principals and assistants were interviewed. The following excerpts from the principals' interviews best describe the system:

Ste-Anne's Principal: I'm the principal of the whole school. The senior teacher is the "vice-principal in charge of French instruction." I have no authority over the curriculum in the bilingual classes. But I am in charge of the safety, discipline, attendance, and overall administration, although she keeps the bilingual class records and reports to the bilingual inspector. I'm responsible only to the English inspector.

St. Anthony's Principal: It's like two schools, really. Mother Prévost has complete authority over the bilingual classes. I'm the overall principal...discipline is my problem....

The dual inspectorate added yet another level of conflict agents. Inspectors were appointed by the Department of Education to oversee the curriculum and administrative aspects of the Education Act. In a district with French schools or panels, one inspector was responsible for the French program, another for the English program. Based on a majority formula set by precedence, one inspector assumed responsibility for the administration of the district and the curricula problems of his linguistic group, the other being limited to the curricula problems of the other linguistic group.

In Tecumseh, where approximately 70 percent of the enrolment was in English classes in 1965, the English inspector assumed the overall responsibility for the administration of the district. In the fifties, when the proportions were reversed (see Figure 6), the administration was under the office of the French inspector. The formation of a County Board in 1969 led to a slightly different arrangement, though the fact that there was still a superintendent for French-language schools and panels maintained the conflict agent characteristic of the position. Essex County separate schools, including those in Tecumseh, now operate under a superintendent of education. Three assistant superintendents relate directly to local schools, two to English schools and one to French schools (Essex County Roman Catholic Separate School Board 1973).

Certain positions within the Department of Education also carried a linguistic component and thus functioned as conflict agents. In 1973, a list of these and related positions was circulated among Franco-Ontarians involved in education.

The Conflict Parties

No less than ninety-four people in positions referred to as "Personnel cadre agrée par le Ministere de l'Education dè l'Ontario et préposé aux écoles de langue française," were listed in this document (Le Conseil supérieur des écoles de langue française 1973).

The connections between these appointments and French Catholic interests were amply illustrated by an article in a 1966 edition of the monthly bulletin of L'Association canadienne française d'Education d'Ontario. The article drew attention to the fact that several recent appointments enlarged "our representation" and could help Franco-Ontarians to see some of their demands realized (*La Vie Franco-Ontarienne* 1966).

The positions of bilingual and English teacher, of bilingual and English principal or senior teacher, of French and English superintendent, and of various appointees in the Department of Education were designated as conflict agents. Whether or not the conflict agent component of these positions was actually used depended on two factors. First, the idiosyncracies of individual incumbents would have some influence. A particular teacher or principal might choose to ignore or might be unaware of this component. There was less chance that a principal or superintendent would take this route as the conflict-agent function was more obvious in these positions; their appointments were made with a recognition of the parties involved and the advantages of representation. Second, apart from individual whims, the variables of the conflict system would influence the extent to which the conflict-agent component was exercised. The very presence of conflict agents is an indicator of institutionalized or regulated conflict.

As with conflict agencies, there was an absence of English Protestant conflict agents. This was due, of course, to the fact that the French panels operated within the separate school system. Locally, there was simply no contact between Catholic and Protestant within the school system. Only at the departmental level might one identify agents associated with each of the three parties French Catholic, English Catholic, and English Protestant.

The Political System. Although school boards are part of the school system, their structure dictates that, for the purposes of locating conflict agents, they are better dealt with as political bodies. It was the structural similarity between the boards and the town council that minimized the possibility of Linguistic-religious conflict agents emerging. The town council has been characterized as contributing to association, and though the school boards are dissociative in the religious sphere, the separate school board was associative in the linguistic cleavage within the Catholic party. Positions on the boards and the council were elected at large; there was no ward system. In contrast with the school system, there were no French or English positions. Members of these political bodies found themselves dealing with all factions to gain and remain in office. Thus, there was no conflict-agent component associated with these positions through their corresponding role sets.

However, a conflict-agent component could be introduced to any of these positions in three ways. First, the status-set of a particular incumbent on a school board or on the town council could introduce the component. Second, given the unequal distribution of party members over the eleven polling divisions, a particular incumbent could either campaign as a representative of party interests or, in spite of himself or herself, poll heavily in certain divisions and be perceived by the voters as representing party interests. Third, as noted previously, language, religion, and residence were partly taken into account by council members in making appointments to municipal boards and commissions.

As would be expected, conflict agents representing linguistic religious interests were not to be found on the public school board. All five members were English Protestants and, with the exception of a few French and English Catholics who were public school supporters, the board operated within the limits of the English Protestant category. It was in the separate school board that the possibility of French and English Catholic conflict agents arose. Of the six separate school board members elected for the 1966-67 term, prior to consolidation, four were Franco-Ontarians and two were English Catholics. The status-set that each brought to the position of board member included his linguistic identity as well as possible memberships in conflict agencies.

During the 1965 election campaign, separate school board candidates emphasized educational and religious interests. No candidate publicly introduced linguistic interests into the campaign. However, the board itself was affiliated with both the Ontario Separate School Trustees' Association (O.S.S.T.A.) and L'Association des Commissions des écoles bilingues d'Ontario (A.C.E.B.0.). The English-speaking members attended only the English O.S.S.T.A. meetings. The remaining four bilingual French-speakers attended meetings of both associations. One member held a position on the provincial executive of the French A.C.E.B.0., and another had received an award of merit from this association. Three of the French-speaking members were also affiliated with local conflict agencies, the S.S.J.B., and the A.P.I. Through membership in such associations, which tied people to the interests of conflict parties, a particular school board member could introduce a conflict-agent component to his or her position on the board. Whether the component was activated or not depended on the incumbent and the variables of the conflict situation.

School consolidation changed this picture somewhat. In 1973, the fourteen members of the county school board represented much larger school districts than those which were administered by the previously locally based boards. Tecumseh was included with St. Clair Beach and Sandwich South Township, and this district sent two representatives to the county board. It so happened that in 1973 both were residents of Tecumseh. The potential conflict-agent component remained; one of the members was viewed locally as representing English Catholic interests, the other, Ste-Anne's parish priest, was viewed by some, but by no means all, as representing Francophone interests. Of equal, if not more, significance for the local conflict system was that issues involving linguistic and religious interests were moved to an extra local-body, thereby decreasing their visibility locally and contributing to an increasing lack of local interest in such issues.

Conflict-agent components were also introduced into positions on the town council in the same manner. In 1966, all five members of the council were Catholic; two were English-speaking, three French-speaking. Two of the French-speaking members belonged to local conflict agencies; one of the English-speaking councillors was a member of a local conflict agency. As in the school board election, none of the candidates publicly campaigned on linguistic-religious issues. In fact, one candidate made a special plea to the voters to avoid viewing the election in linguistic-religious terms. For the first time in the memory of the citizens, campaign meetings were held in the English as well as the French side of town.

In spite of these efforts, the voting patterns previously examined suggested that linguistic-religious interests played a part. It was noted that candidates calculated expected votes on a linguistic-religious basis and that one English Catholic candidate was singled out by a few members of the English Protestant sub-community to represent their interests.

It would not have followed that a candidate receiving heavy support from one of the three conflict parties automatically became a conflict agent. The voting patterns only provided a basis from which a particular member of the town council might act as a conflict agent given certain issues and conditions. There was no absolute coincidence between party membership and voting patterns as each member of the council received some support from all three parties and was obligated to act accordingly. The primary issues facing the council were community-wide and could only, with difficulty, be interpreted in linguistic or religious terms.

The Church. As with the public school board, the one Protestant church in Tecumseh contained no conflict agents in the context under investigation. The Catholic church, because of its associative nature within the Catholic category, was also void of conflict agents. Most of the party interests within the parish were aggregated and articulated by conflict agencies. The clergy could become conflict agents, but, in 1966, in Tecumseh all three clergy were Franco-Ontarians. There was no tradition of appointing French and English priests. If an attempt were made to maintain a linguistic balance in clerical appointments, the possibility of conflict agents would increase considerably and could take on a structure similar to that in the school system.

It was in the school system that conflict agents were readily identified, especially at the administrative level. To a lesser extent, conflict agents were apparent on the separate school board. The phenomenon all but disappeared on the town council, with the exception of special boards and commissions, and was absent in the parish. The difference between the school and the remaining bodies referred to is that positions in the school system carried a conflict-agent component, regardless of the incumbent, through associated role-sets. School board, town council, and church positions could only develop a conflict-agent component through the status-sets of particular incumbents.

We have now established the existence of two of the conditions required for a state of social conflict to obtain in Tecumseh. First, there were three social categories or conflict parties based on linguistic and religious affiliations. These were shown to be more than mere aggregates. Second, the three conflict parties were interacting in terms of French Catholic, English Catholic, and English Protestant interests.

The interaction among the parties took place through conflict agencies and agents. These were the mediating links, the indicators of interaction (Drake 1957, p. 162; Williams 1957, p. 451). There is, however, an important difference between conflict agencies and agents. Certain organizations are generated by conflict parties as agencies defining and representing party interests. As organizations recruit from each party, they remain independent of other parties in a dispute. In contrast, conflict agents presuppose structures which supersede and include the disputants. The school system, for example, is common ground. The Essex County Roman Catholic Separate School Board is Catholic, but neither French nor English. The Department of Education is neither French nor English, Catholic nor Protestant. The conflict-agent function is the result of role-sets related to positions in these structures and the status-sets which the incumbents carry into the positions. The presence of conflict agents, though an indicator of inter-party interaction, is also an indicator that the conflict is regulated or institutionalized to the extent that the existence and claims of the respective parties are recognized.

This discussion brings to mind another aspect of the connections among the parties that would appear to be a prerequisite for social conflict. Earlier I stated that conflict requires community. In a recent article, Professor Robin Williams Jr. suggested that parties to a conflict situation show an interdependence "in activities that are necessary for the gratification of vital needs or for the expression or maintenance of crucial values and beliefs" (Williams 1972, p. 18). This would appear to have been the case in Tecumseh. In school, parish, and in politics, the active participation of each of the parties was necessary in order to carry on the collective enterprise at a level beyond the interests of each party.

Scarcity and Incompatibility.

It is from conditions of scarcity and incompatibility that the issues arise over which conflict episodes take place. Conflicts involve "attempts to gain control over scarce resources and positions or to influence behavior in certain directions" (Mack and Snyder 1957, p. 219). Subjectively, conflicts do not take place over boundary maintenance, but over values, resources, and desirable positions within the social structure.

Resource scarcity only exists because there is more than one party. That is, if there were only a single school system on which no special linguistic or religious demands were made, there would be no scarcity of resources. The scarcity, in this sense, is a result of two, and to some extent, three sub-systems competing for the educational dollar. Scarcity is a consequence of an unequal distribution of resources among parties rather than a necessarily absolute or objective state. The parties do not arise because of scarcity; scarcity arises because of a multiplicity of demands on a limited resource. Position scarcity also presupposes the existence of parties and the ascription of positions according to party membership. If party membership is a criterion for the distribution of positions in the social structure, an unequal distribution of status and power is implied.

The Conflict Parties

Position and Resource Scarcity. Position and resource scarcity are not necessarily mutually exclusive categories. Status and power may also be considered as resources and, as such, the distribution of positions according to party membership implies attempts to gain these resources as a possible focus of conflict systems. Status and power are as necessary as financial resources as a means to attain goals.

Within the context of French-English relations in Ontario, attempts on the part of Franco-Ontarians to gain or increase power took place at two levels of organization. First, there was a push to gain collective power through demands for positions within certain institutional structures. Frequent demands for Franco-Ontarian representation on appointed bodies and to appointed offices within the federal government appeared in Ottawa's *Le Droit*. Generally, in these requests comparisons were made to the English-speaking representation from Quebec:

> Modest and patient, the Franco-Ontarians remain content with two seats in the Upper Chamber when their number demands a better representation. Proportionately, Franco-Ontarians are as numerous in Ontario (10.39 percent in the last census) as are English-speakers in Quebec (10.78 percent)....
> (*Le Droit* 1966)

Similar attempts may be noted in the field of education. In October, 1965, for example, the directors of L'Association canadienne-française d'Education d'Ontario met with the Ministry of Education Council on Orientation and Development. Among the items discussed was a proposed decentralization of departmental administrative machinery. According to a report on the meeting, in order for decentralization

> ...to be acceptable to Franco-Ontarians provision must be made for certain nominations [of Franco-Ontarians] within various branches of the Ministry.
> (*La Vie Franco-Ontarienne* 1966, p.2)

135

Demands for positions in the Department of Education also appeared in the resolutions of the 1966 General Congress of L'Association d'Education, and in a brief presented to the provincial government's Hall Commission on Education (*La Vie Franco-Ontarienne* 1966, pp. 12, 14).

From observable demands of this type, it may be inferred that there was a condition of resource scarcity, with attempts by both parties to hold on to or gain positions of power within the educational and political spheres. English Catholics made similar demands on the educational system. According to an officer of the Ontario English Catholic Education Association, demands for more English Catholic representation on Department of Education policy groups is one of the Association's "main concerns." It should be noted that these demands are directed toward the government and, in this sense, the government is viewed as representing English Protestant interests.

At the local level, there was a more equal distribution of positions of influence in church, school, and municipal politics. If anything, there was a feeling among English Protestants that they were underrepresented in municipal politics, as was shown in the earlier comments on "the French clique" and attempts to support an English Catholic for municipal office. The problem of scarcity from a local point of view focused more on the unequal distribution of financial resources between the separate and public school systems and between French and English panels within the separate system.

The second level refers to individual rather than collective demands for status and power. Within the occupational structure, locally, provincially, and nationally, Catholics tended to remain in lower-status occupations more so than Protestants, and French-speakers were more predominant at the lower-status levels than English-speakers. Tables 14 and 15 demonstrated the unequal distribution of status and income in the membership of the three conflict parties. English Protestants ranked highest, followed by English and French Catholics.

This second level of position scarcity is referred to as "individual" rather than "collective" because the demand is for a distribution of occupations according to achievement as opposed to ascribed characteristics. A Franco-Ontarian does not want to be held back because he is French, nor a Catholic because he is Catholic. Both desire to be treated on an equal basis with English Protestants, given the qualifications. This is in contrast with the demand for collective recognition in institutional structures as French or English Catholics. Certainly, a Franco-Ontarian can move on an equal basis with Anglo-Ontarians if he rejects his identity or "passes." In the course of the field work, I received some reports of Franco-Ontarians changing or anglicizing their names in order to merge into the dominant group.

Some will argue that French Catholics hold lower-income jobs because they are not qualified to do otherwise. From the point of view of this analysis, it is of little importance why French Catholics find themselves in this position. What is relevant is that there is a condition of position and resource scarcity among the three parties under analysis.

Incompatible Values. Historically, Anglophones have assumed an assimilationist position; Francophones have tended toward separation. Taken to the extreme, the two positions are incompatible. The dialogue has resulted in a type of pluralism adhered to by a majority of the members of all parties. Issues have focused on types of pluralism and the degree of pluralism accepted by one side or demanded by the other. This has been especially true in Ontario where Franco-Ontarians have generally held a pan-Canadian view of the position of French vis-à-vis English Canada. The incompatibility is much more apparent in the dialogue between Quebec and Canada where the separatist position is clearly articulated.

The incompatibility of positions within the pluralistic orientation is subtly buried in the very generality of pluralism itself. The Anglo-Ontarian position implies a pluralism where all cultures, including French Canada, should be permitted to maintain their heritage, thereby contributing to the greater whole. The greater whole is viewed as an Anglophone or Canadian culture. Franco-Ontarians, in contrast, view the greater whole as a cooperative venture between two cultures, implying a degree of structural pluralism which the

137

Anglophone finds difficult to accept and, at times, to comprehend.

These differences were apparent in Tecumseh. A general, open question concerning biculturalism and bilingualism was asked in all interviews of members of conflict agencies and conflict agents. It should be recalled that these interviews were primarily to identify conflict agents and agencies, and were not intended to sample the value positions of the community as a whole. In any case, of the forty-one respondents interviewed, twenty-four were French Catholics, twelve were English Catholics, and five were English Protestants. All accepted a pluralistic position on French-English relations. Contrary to what might be expected, although consistent with the close contact between French and English Catholics, the French Catholic and English Protestant views were closer than the French and English Catholic views.

The following is an excerpt from an interview with a member of the public school board:

> I'd hate to lose French Canada. I would like my children to learn French in schools....This is what I would like...actually we should come up with a solution to the problem and both be able to carry on our own traditions in harmony. I'd hate to see the French people told that they had to speak English all the time and that's that.

Another member of the public school board said that:

> The only way for harmony is definitely to recognize French culture as a part of Canada. I would very much like to see French taught in the public schools.

Compare these to the following statement made by the president of L'Association St-Jean-Baptiste de l'Ouest d'Ontario:

> We must work hand in hand, arm in arm, as two groups each with our own identity...the English

should learn French and, of course, we learn English. Then we can work together.

In a similar vein, a Franco-Ontarian school teacher felt that:

> ...both groups should meet somewhere in the middle without losing their own identities. Complete separation would prevent a unity, but we should be able to reach some unity on the basis that we are all Canadian. If a student is French Canadian, he should attend a French school. You can't be both. A person owes his loyalty to his own culture.

In contrast was the following view held by an English Catholic educational official:

> I think it's good and valuable to maintain different cultures — the mosaic idea, each contributes to the total. Theoretically, it's a good idea. But practically, what if you have different languages and different goals within one nation? There is certainly more possibility for conflict and dissension. This isn't good. Different languages means a lack of communication.

English Catholics do not generalize their views on language to Protestant-Catholic relations. The same respondent was asked, "What about religious differences, should we all be of one religion?" He replied:

> I don't think that's the same thing. Different religions don't prevent communication and cooperation like different languages. The cooperation between us and the public school board in Windsor is very, very good for example.

An English Catholic school teacher expressed a similar opinion:

I have my doubts whether duality will work...I wonder if they [French-speakers] put the country or the
language first. The country must come first.

A prominent English Catholic member of Ste-Anne's parish
commented:

I'm favourable to French schools, the usual classes
though [referring to English and French panels in
contrast with French schools as such]. French will
inevitably disappear anyway.

The English Protestant tendency to agree with the
French Catholic view is partly a result of their lack of contact
in areas other than that of municipal politics. They are less
tolerant, however, of the Catholic position on education.
Opinions range from mere acceptance — "separate schools are
a fact of life; it's accepted whether we approve or not" — to
frank expressions of disagreement:

They have a right to separate schools, but not to
equal grants from my point of view. They chose to
opt out of the public system from the beginning.

The public school taxes are lower because we get, up
until recently, the biggest hunk of the bounty from
the province. Recently, Robarts [the provincial
premier] has changed this and now Catholics are
getting an equal amount. I think this is wrong.
This is really wrong because we are operating a
public school system and the Catholics can operate
their own if they want to, but we should put all our
resources into the public system.

There was a divergence of opinion within each group as
well as between groups. With only forty-one respondents who
were not primarily selected for a sampling of opinion, the
above comments are presented as illustrating the tendencies
within each party toward types of orientations. Indeed, the
most outright assimilationist of all the respondents was a

Franco-Ontarian teacher in the English panel. It may be concluded from these data, however, that there were differing value positions and that these positions followed party membership.

We now have a picture of the anatomy or structure of the conflict situation in Tecumseh on French-English relations. Language and religion intersected to form three social categories or conflict parties. These parties exhibited a degree of interdependence and they interacted with each other through the medium of conflict agencies and agents. Furthermore, a condition of value incompatibility and resource scarcity obtained among the three parties. It was out of this condition that the issues over which people found themselves in conflict were generated. What remains to be done now is to examine the dynamics of the conflict system; this will be the topic of the next chapter.

Chapter Six

The Conflict System

Social conflict was defined as a type of interaction resulting from a particular arrangement of social categories and related interests. With this in mind, the relationships among the three categories in Tecumseh were such that a state of conflict existed. To stop here would leave us with less than a complete picture. The picture we have so far is static, a single frame in which we can see the parties and the relationships that obtain among them. We have yet to deal with their interaction as conflict parties.

Some social scientists have made a distinction between statics and dynamics. J.A. Schumpeter in his *History of Economic Analysis* presented this distinction in the following manner:

> By static analysis we mean a *method* of dealing with economic phenomena that tries to establish relations between elements of the economic system — prices and quantities of commodities — all of which...refer to the same point in time....But the elements of the economic system that interact at a given point of time are evidently the result of preceding configurations; and the way itself in which they interact is not less evidently influenced by what people expect future configurations to be....Hence we are led to take into account past and (expected) future values of our variables, lags, sequences, rates of change, cumulative magnitudes, expectations, and so on. The *methods* that aim at doing this constitute economic dynamics.
> (Schumpeter, 1954, p. 963)

Our task, therefore, is to deal with the dynamics of the system as constructed. Given that a state of conflict existed among three identified collections of people, we must now ask what

changes have taken place in their relationships over time. It is
known that some conflicts are more intense than others and
that any given conflict may exhibit a greater level of intensity
at one time than at another. Accordingly our questions must
be directed toward variations in the conflict under examination and the conditions which account for these variations.

These questions suggest that we observe the specific issues over which interaction among the parties took place. A
conflict system is brought into action only insofar as the members of the participating parties perceive certain events as
challenging their continued existence, their rights, or previously defined agreements. Such events are the issues over
which conflicts take place. Having identified the issues, we
must then decide what is the form and content of the interaction over the issues, and to what extent conflict agencies and
agents are mobilized. In addition, there is the question of the
extent to which the interaction is maintained at the local level,
and to which previously arrived at rules governing the conflict
are adhered to or changed. These questions and others are the
indicators of process.

The Issues

As noted in the previous chapter, any number of social situations may generate issues bringing some sector of the conflict
system into action. The refusal of a federal government
agency to serve a Francophone in his or her own language,
placing a bilingual sign on the lawn in front of the parish
church, or assigning an Anglophone altar boy to the French-
language Mass are all specific issues at the local level. These
and others, trivial though they may appear, bring conflict
agencies and agents into play, usually within a framework of
established rules for dealing with just such events.
Presumably some issues are more important than others; that
is, some events present a greater perceived threat to a party's
legitimacy, rights or interests. The history of the relationships
among the three parties points to politics, religion, and education as the spheres of activity that generate the most salient
issues.

While discussing issues related to the conflict system, one should keep in mind that the citizens of Tecumseh participate in other systems as well. There are other configurations of people in roles and groups that respond to issues divorced from French-English or Catholic-Protestant interests. One such set of issues would be that related to overall community concerns, with the municipality as the focus. Taxes, industrial development, recreation, pollution, road management, and so on are issues of this type. Of course, there is nothing intrinsic in these particular issues to prevent them from being cast in terms of the conflict under study.

The important point is that we might well expect that certain issues related to the community as a whole would transcend religious and linguistic interests.

With the aim of obtaining data on the relative importance of community and religious-linguistic issues to Tecumseh residents, respondents in the 1966 sample were asked to rank a set of six issues, three of which referred to the community as a whole, the remaining three to linguistic and religious interests. These six issues, presented to each respondent on a card, a facsimile of which appears below, were chosen, from observations and interviews, as the issues most frequently discussed at that time.

Issue Ranking Card

On this card is a list of current issues in Tecumseh. Would you please rank these in their order of importance to you? That is, place a (1) beside the issue you believe to be the most important; a (2) beside the next most important, and so on down to a (6) beside the least important.

Issues   Rank

1. Industrial development   _____
2. Extension of government support _____
   to Catholic schools up to grade thirteen
3. Juvenile delinquency   _____
4. Bilingual classes for French-speaking _____
   children from Kindergarten to grade thirteen
5. Sewage treatment facilities   _____
6. Equalization of income for public _____
   and separate schools

Items 1, 3, and 5 were taken as community-wide issues; items 2, 4, and 6 as religious-linguistic issues. The data were summarized by adding the rank scores for each set of issues; the lower the total, the more important the issue or set of issues. The sum of the assigned ranks for the religious-linguistic issues was 1,723 and for the community-wide issues, 1,614. A summary measure for comparison was obtained by dividing these totals by the total number of respondents (155). The result, rounded off, yielded the average rank score for each item and set of items. The average for the linguistic-religious items was eleven, and for the community wide issues, ten. Disregarding party membership, the sample tended to view community-wide issues as slightly more important than religious-linguistic issues. An analysis of the averages according to party membership indicated that this was due to the much heavier weight placed on community-wide issues by English-speakers.

As Table 24 shows, Anglophones, both Catholic and Protestant, and English Protestants ranked community-wide issues as much more important than did Francophones. French Catholics tended to place a slightly greater importance on religious-linguistic issues than English Catholics, though both Catholic categories exhibited more of a balance between the two sets of issues than did English Protestants. The differences between French and English Catholics may be analyzed further by examining the response of each to single issues. In Tables 25 to 27, respondents who assigned a rank of

1, 2, or 3 to an issue were classified as designating that issue more important than those assigning a rank of 4, 5 or 6.

First, looking at the results for the Catholic category as a whole, the secondary school issue (Table 27) appeared to be the most important, with the equalization of income for separate schools (Table 26) next, and the extension of bilingual classes (Table 25) least important. The linguistic categories were about equal in their response to the secondary school issue, with French Catholics ranking equalization of income only slightly higher and, as might be expected, the language issue considerably higher than English Catholics ranked it. Even here French Catholics split on the relative importance assigned to the language issue.

Apart from identifying the issues and their relative importance to Tecumseh residents, two characteristics of the conflict system are suggested by these data. However, the ranking does not imply that given an issue — for example, the extension of Catholic education to grade thirteen — the English Protestant party will not respond in opposition. It implies only that when forced to make a choice, the Protestant is more likely to consider this issue of less importance than, say, industrial development.

The first characteristic of the conflict system revealed by these data is the possibility that a commitment to community-wide issues may well modify the extent to which people in Tecumseh will involve themselves over religious-linguistic issues. James Coleman in his analysis of community conflict suggests as much (1957, p.21). Secondly, it is possible to obtain some impression of the extent to which the presence of English Catholics might modify the conflict relations around certain issues. The members of this category tend to ally with English Protestants on language issues and with French Catholics on religious issues. Thus, seldom was there a single issue where the opposing groups were "pure" in terms of party membership. We will return to these characteristics later.

Table 24
A Comparison of Average Ranking scores for Religious-Linguistic and Community-Wide Issues by Membership in Conflict Parties

Parties	Religious-linguistic Issues	Community-wide Issues
Set no. 1		
French Catholics	10	11
English Catholics	11	10
English Protestants	14	7
Set no.2		
Catholics	10	11
Protestants	14	7
Francophones	10	11
Anglophones	12	9

Table 25
French and English Catholic Ranking of the Issue "Bilingual
Classes for French-Speaking Children to Grade Thirteen" in
Relation to Five Other Issues

| | Rank Assigned | | |
Party	Percent more important	Percent less important	Total
French Catholic	50.0	50.0	100.0
English Catholic	17.0	83.0	100.0
Total	36.0	64.0	100.0[a]

[a]Number, 121; no answer, 10.

Table 26
French and English Catholic Ranking of the Issue "Equal
Grants for Public and Separate Schools"
in Relation to Five Other Issues

Party	Percent more important	Percent less important	Total
French Catholic	56.0	44.0	100.0
English Catholic	52.0	48.0	100.0
Total	54.0	46.0	100.0[a]

[a]Number, 121; no answer, 10.

Table 27
French and English Catholic Ranking of the Issue "Extension
of Government Support to Catholic Schools up to Grade
Thirteen" in Relation to Five Other Issues

Party	Percent more important	Percent less important	Total
French Catholic	70.0	30.0	100.0
English Catholic	71.0	29.0	100.0
Total	70.0	30.0	100.0[a]

[a]Number, 121; no answer, 10.

Issues in Process

Now that we have some notion of the major issues, we are
ready to examine the interaction of the conflict parties. I will
limit the discussion to issues related to education. There is
considerable historical justification for this, as education has
been one of the most prominent issues in French-English relations both inside and outside Quebec. I will deal with the
Catholic school and the French school issues separately keeping the connections between the two issues in mind.

Catholic Schools

The two major concerns of Ontario Catholics regarding their
schools are the issues of equalization of income at the elementary level and the extension of public schooling for Catholics to
grade thirteen, the final year of secondary education. Though
the first issue has been a component of Protestant-Catholic
relations since the early days of Upper Canada, Catholics have

made considerable progress in achieving their objectives. The second issue is more recent and far more salient at the moment. Referring to Tables 26 and 27, 54 percent of Tecumseh Catholics ranked the first issue highly, while 70 percent so ranked the second issue. Furthermore, the difference in emphasis according to language was minimal. The Catholic school issues bring both Francophone and Anglophone Catholics together in opposition to Anglophone Protestants. Only recently, a topic for later discussion, have Francophone Catholics in Ontario separated linguistic from religious interests in the school debate.

The Bases of Catholic Schools. As we saw in Chapter 2, the Scott Act of 1863 provided the legal basis from which Catholic schools in Ontario were to develop after Confederation. As the Act was embodied in Section 93 of the British North America Act, Catholic schools were not allocated corporation taxes nor was the development of secondary schools provided for. Given the legitimacy of Catholic education per se, although limited in resources and in scope, a system for dealing with Catholic claims developed between the Government of Ontario (regardless of the party in power and acting as the spokespeople for Protestant opposition) and representatives of Catholic interests. During the early years of Confederation, the presence of such conflict agents as the Archbishop of Toronto, representatives of the separate school boards sitting on public high school boards, and Catholic members of the legislature and cabinet, were able to communicate Catholic interests and demands. In effect, the relationship between Catholic and Protestant interests was fairly well institutionalized at the turn of the century.

In this system of relationships, the government played a dual role. Decisions on the amount of recognition and resources to be allocated to Catholic schools lay in the hands of the government. Thus, both Catholic and Protestant agencies had to deal with the government, Catholics in terms of their demands and Protestants in terms of their opposition to those demands. In this sense the government acted as a third party to the conflict, as a mediator. However, the government also represented the position of the Protestant majority in the province. It did not act merely as the recipient of Protestant and Catholic claims for educational resources. It was also the custodian of a public school system designated as Protestant in orientation. Catholics were, therefore, placed in a position where they had to claim concessions from the generally accepted system, whereas Protestants defended this system against Catholic threats. In this sense, the government was a conflict agency generated by a Protestant population who controlled the political, economic, and social reality.

These contradictory roles of government — logically, one cannot be a mediator and a party to a conflict simultaneously — had several consequences. The third-party role enabled a system of conflict agents to develop within the administration dealing with the educational legislation. That is, within the ministry and cabinet, Catholics were represented, giving explicit recognition to their legitimacy and claims. This, too, provided a means of "visibility management." The visibility of specific claims and issues generated could be kept within the framework of the administration of education and thereby off the floor of the legislature and out of the public eye. It simply permitted a means of further institutionalizing the conflict system.

The conflict agency role comes to the fore as issues become more visible to the public at large. If a minority presses its claims beyond the limits that can be dealt with administratively or if the majority moves to abrogate previous agreements, issues are likely to move from the administrative to the political sphere of government. The government then assumes the role of conflict agency, taking either a defensive or an offensive stand on minority claims. In this case, it is at such times that Catholic school demands are likely to become election issues. In effect the conflict system has been slightly deinstitutionalized.

Up to the turn of the century, the Catholic school issue was in the main dealt with administratively, with the bishops playing the major role on behalf of Catholic interests. By 1928, the Catholic claims for redistribution of educational resources still had not been recognized, although they had won the right to operate "continuation classes" for the first two years of a high school program in municipalities where high schools did not exist.[1]

It was at this time that the conflict entered a new phase with greater involvement of Catholics and an increase in the presentation of demands. Several factors, both external and internal to the conflict system, contributed to this increase in intensity. Externally, demands for mass education before the turn of the century were fairly low, especially beyond the elementary level. The rapid urbanization and industrialization of Canada after 1900 placed demands on local educational systems which the public schools with their superior resources were able to meet. The limitations on separate school financing prevented Catholics from meeting these demands within their own system. As secondary schooling became more important if one were to make an adequate income, Catholics realized they would have to increase their efforts to prepare their separate system to take part in the new opportunities offered by a developing economy. The previous agreement had to be challenged, thereby de-institutionalizing and escalating the conflict.

Related to these external changes was the changing role of the laity in the Roman Catholic church in Canada. The laity was assuming a more active decision-making role within the church. In addition, there were the real effects of the tax burden of maintaining and improving a Catholic education system under limitations not imposed on the majority population. The conflict was no longer purely a matter for bishops and cabinet ministers. The organization of the Catholic Taxpayers' Association of Ontario, a new conflict agency, began in the fall of 1931. The involvement of the Catholic laity moved the focus from the previous system of conflict agents within the government to the political level, intensifying local activity.

Another external factor of considerable import was the fact that the French-language issue in Ontario schools was brought to a temporary conclusion in 1927 following seventeen

---

1. This, by the way, is the basis from which grades nine and ten are operated in Tecumseh under the Essex County Roman Catholic Separate School Board. In the 1896 legislation, the government did not specify separate school boards, but referred to "school boards" only. This is another method of "visibility management" related to the third party role of government.

years of bitter relationships between Francophone and Anglophone Catholics. By 1928 the two were again prepared to join in their struggle with the government over Catholic school demands. In 1928, L'Association canadienne-française d'éducation d'Ontario expressed its willingness to cooperate with English Catholics to secure additional revenue for separate schools (Walker 1964, p. 349). The Tecumseh Separate School Board had sent four delegates to the meeting at which this decision was made (Minutes, Tecumseh Separate School Board 1928). La Société St-Jean-Baptiste encouraged Franco-Ontarians to participate in the activities of the Catholic Taxpayers' Association (*La Feuille d'Erable*, Tecumseh 1933). By 1934, L'Association canadienne-française d'éducation d'Ontario voted to associate itself with the Catholic Taxpayers' Association.

It should be noted that the great majority of the citizens of Tecumseh during this period were Francophone and Catholic. In 1921, 86 percent of Tecumseh's population was of French origin; 94 percent was Catholic. The dilution of the town's population did not begin until the 1940's. Language, religion, and community thus coincided during this phase of the conflict over Catholic school demands. Though the major decisions regarding Catholic education were made outside the community, a French Catholic community faced a hostile English Protestant province.

The involvement of Tecumseh citizens at this time was reflected in the minutes of the Tecumseh Separate School Board and on the pages of its local newspaper, *La Feuille d'Erable*. The problem of financing its separate schools increased year by year during the thirties, culminating in the closing of the schools for a brief period in 1936 (Minutes, Tecumseh Separate School Board 1936). One cannot ignore the effect of the Depression as another external factor on these issues.

At this time, the Tecumseh board was demanding increased revenue for its schools. Petitions from many Catholic parishes were sent to the provincial premier, followed by counter-petitions from the Protestants. The issue was raised again by both sides during the 1933 provincial election and two years later delegations from both parties met the new premier. Eventually in 1936, Catholic claims were recognized through increases in departmental grants to separate schools. This action finally returned the issue to the administrative level and out of public view. By 1942, a salaried official of the Catholic party was acting as a liaison between the Catholic party, the Department of Education, and the government. His role as a conflict agent was recognized by both parties (Walker 1964, pp. 481-482).

The network of agencies and agents operated fairly well until the mid-sixties. The complex of local, regional, and provincial conflict agencies representing Catholic interests was described in Chapter 5. The question of an equitable income for Catholic education was, for the most part, mediated administratively through departmental regulations within the framework of existing legislation. When legislation was deemed necessary, as was the case in 1963 when the Ontario Foundation Tax Plan was introduced, specific reference to separate schools was omitted — another example of issue "visibility management."

Briefs presented by Catholic conflict agencies during this period were inclined to argue for additional funds within the existing framework. Catholic education was gaining, but the two basic demands of its proponents — equal resources and extension of the system to the end of high school — had not been met.

The Pressure of the Sixties. Once again, a number of external events suggested that the dialogue could not be completely maintained within the labyrinth of organizations and the Department of Education. Since the mid-forties, an ever-increasing premium had been placed on education as the means to opportunity and mobility. Generally, Catholic incomes in Canada have been lower than Protestant incomes (Porter 1965, pp. 98-103). This was most certainly the case in Tecumseh. A Catholic would be more likely to attribute this problem to a lack of educational opportunities in a system hamstrung by the Protestant majority than to any cultural explanation such as "the Protestant work ethic." The 1863 legislation determined that Catholics would have to become

Protestants or at best, simply secularized, if they were to benefit from a completely publicly financed education system.

Education itself, Catholic and non-Catholic, was responding to the main trends in the society at large. Professionalization, bureaucratization, and an increasing sophistication in educational technology all contributed to soaring costs which, for Catholics in towns like Tecumseh, meant a far greater tax burden than that assumed by public school supporters. To add to the financial burden and in response to the premium placed on education, Catholics throughout Ontario began to erect parochial secondary schools. Ste-Anne's High School in Tecumseh was one of these. The professionalization of education meant more lay teachers and higher salaries. No longer could Catholics cut costs through the services of religious orders.

Demographic factors also contributed to a renewal of the Catholic school issue. Catholic and public school systems alike experienced pressure from increased numbers of school-age children during the late fifties and early sixties. In addition, the Catholic population had increased in Ontario by one-third between 1961 and 1971. Its proportion to the total population had increased 3.3 percent during the same period. Nor can one underestimate the influence of the stress placed on minority rights during the mid-sixties and the newly accepted style of middle-class protest, new only in that it had been absent from the public eye for two decades and tended to involve the more youthful members of society.

To these, we may add two more specific events. By the late sixties most local school boards in Ontario had been consolidated at the county level, though religious and linguistic divisions remained. Catholics rightly saw consolidation as one way to deal with financial problems. This had the effect of bringing the whole issue once more into public view. In June, 1968 the Department of Education announced that separate schools would be consolidated into county units (*The Windsor Star* 1968). Finally, *Living and Learning*, the Hall-Denis Report on education in Ontario suggested several reforms for Catholic education. This study, commissioned by the government and released in the late sixties, further contributed to the visibility of the issue.

The Conflict System

In Tecumseh in the mid-sixties, the two C.P.T.A.'s and the A.P.I., and, to a certain extent, the separate school board were the local organizational mechanisms available to the Catholic laity on the school issue. In the vertical system, the decision making and the confrontation between Protestant and Catholic took place at the provincial level. Locally, these organizations or conflict agencies could do no more than discuss the issues and forward resolutions and delegates to regional and provincial bodies. In addition, there was local, individual representation on such bodies as the Ontario Separate School Trustees' Association and various teachers' organizations.

This system could not contain the issues against the various external pressures discussed above. Locally, the financial burden was becoming exceptionally difficult for individual families especially those with children of high school age. The separate school board itself was dubious of its ability to maintain grades nine and ten, its "continuation classes." As noted earlier, these secondary school years had to be maintained out of elementary school grants. Some alleviation of costs had been worked out by using the intermediate school building for grades seven and eight as well as the two "continuation classes." Also, since it was only across the street from Ste-Anne's High School, the parochial school could use some of their facilities to reduce parish capital and operating costs. But these measures were insufficient in the face of overwhelming costs and the generally lower incomes of Catholics in Tecumseh compared to non-Catholics.

In 1965 and 1966, the provincial body of the C.P.T.A.'s was already attempting to gather local support for a renewed assault on the government. On March 31, 1966, a group of five teachers, four teaching in the English panel and one teaching in the French panel, called a meeting of teachers, board members, and interested citizens to discuss the problems of Catholic education in Tecumseh. The meeting was not well attended; a handful of teachers, three members of the separate school board, one member of the parish high school board, and two or three citizens were present. Nevertheless, the meeting was the first overt expression of dissatisfaction with the current system of mediating Catholic interests and represented

157

the entry of teachers in their professional capacity into the struggle at the local level.

The major issue discussed at this meeting had to do with a possible union of the intermediate and high schools in terms of a single administration and a greater sharing of facilities. This practice was becoming common in Ontario. In accordance with existing legislation, the two schools would remain separate, one parochial and one tax-supported, though for all practical purposes they would operate as one school. Board members and citizens tended to be suspicious of the teachers' motives, preferring the issues to be dealt with through the C.P.T.A.'s, though all were aware that this was proving quite unsatisfactory. In spite of some objections, the Tecumseh Catholic Education Association was formed at the meeting and agreed to make representation to the two school boards. Although this organization was short-lived, it served to open the issue for discussion at the board level and initiated the involvement of Tecumseh citizens in the issue.

By 1968 Catholic conflict agencies at the diocesan and provincial levels were beginning to press the government harder about secondary schools (*The Windsor Star*, July 11, 1968). Their activities increased the visibility of the issue sufficiently to bring counter-reactions from Protestant groups. At the local level, a delegation of parents met with the new Essex County Roman Catholic School Board in the summer of 1969 to discuss the problems of tax burdens. A decision was taken to maintain grades nine and ten at Ste-Anne's Intermediate School for another year contingent upon the ratepayers' ability and willingness to absorb the cost either by taxation or subscription. Those with children attending the parochial high school also met to deal with diminishing funds. Students picketed parishioners in town, demonstrating their plight and noting that 85 percent of the support for the high school came from 20 percent of the 1200 families involved (*The Windsor Star*, April 29, 1969).

The struggle escalated through to the provincial election in 1971. In May, 1969, the premier of the province stated that the province simply could not afford two complete systems (*The Windsor Star*, May 28, 1969). Several meetings were held in Essex County involving parents from Tecumseh and dealing mainly with the problem of maintaining grades nine and ten. There was considerable resistance to a request from the board for a $150.00 tuition fee per pupil over and above taxes to maintain the system (*The Windsor Star*, September 9, 1969). Through 1969 and into 1970, students became more and more involved in the issue, collecting petitions and holding rallies.

In addition to the counter-actions by the Protestant churches, the Ontario Public School Trustees' Association submitted a brief opposing extension of aid to separate schools. The brief interpreted aid to separate schools as attempts to segregate the school system. Such attempts at segregation according to race, language, colour or creed were referred to as "insidious [and] foreign...to Canadian concepts." The brief also requested that grants to grades nine and ten within the separate systems be cut off and per pupil grants to separate schools be reduced (*The Windsor Star*, January 21, 1970).

Catholic schools became a major issue in the 1971 Ontario provincial election, especially in areas such as Essex County which were heavily populated by Roman Catholics. Tecumseh residents attended a meeting with local candidates in the neighbouring community of Riverside on October 6, 1971. Though the candidates attempted to direct attention toward such issues as pollution or auto insurance, the audience turned the session into a discussion of the Catholic school issue.

The results of this election were analyzed in Chapter 4. Though the Conservative Party was returned to power, 79.3 percent of the Tecumseh voters voted for opposition parties, 50.5 percent for the N.D.P., the only party explicitly to come out in favour of a dual system. With the Conservatives returned to power, there were no significant changes for Catholic schools. The struggle continues.

It should be apparent that the interaction between Protestant and Catholic over this issue took place outside the local milieu. The issue was dealt with in the vertical rather than the horizontal system of community organization. Except for the expression of opinions and, undoubtedly, the occasional argument at the inter-personal level, interaction between Protestant and Catholic was achieved through mass meetings and organizational statements, all directed to the Department of Education and the provincial government. Though this does contribute to a less intense conflict at the local level, it also leads to considerable withdrawal of local citizens from the conflict. The decisions are not in their hands. This tends to promote apathy, so often given as the reason for all organizational failures, over local conflict agencies, C.P.T.A.'s, Home and School Associations and the like.

For the most part, the Catholic protest in Tecumseh involved both Francophones and Anglophones united in a common struggle. Nevertheless, there was some dissension. English Catholics frequently viewed the Francophones' efforts to maintain French-language classes and separate organizations as weakening the common front on the Catholic school issue. Indeed, their reactions were not unlike the reactions of Protestants toward Catholic education. Each saw the minority party as contributing to segregation, in the pejorative sense, and each saw their own position as the truly neutral one on the minority position. These feelings were quite clear in 1957 when Francophone members of the Tecumseh C.P.T.A. withdrew to form their own organization, the A.P.I. One English Catholic expressed his feelings about it in this way:

> Well, if they want to form their own group, that's their business. But this culture bit, I don't go for that; that's not the purpose of the P.T.A. The aim is the children....We're already split into public and separate schools, the children suffer, especially in grades nine and ten. Then when you add the language split, it only gets worse.

A similar comment was made to me by one of the Anglophone teachers attending the meeting to form the Tecumseh Catholic Education Association:

> Our trouble is that we're split two ways; down the middle linguistically with two groups of teachers and across with two boards, one for elementary schools and one for high schools.

French Schools

Early Development. As with Catholic schools, French predated English Protestant schooling in many parts of the region
that was to become Ontario. By Confederation, the relationships between French and English-language schools were at a
relatively high level of institutionalization. Nevertheless, by
not recognizing language rights in the schools, the British
North America Act provided an opening to rescind or limit established use of the French language should the occasion arise.
French-language schools were, at this time, experiencing the
same external pressures as Catholic schools, since, with some
exceptions, most French schools were separate schools. These
pressures increased the visibility of the French schools.

Furthermore, during the late 1870's a Ministry of
Education succeeded the Council of Public Instruction which,
though responsible to the government, had been removed from
the political process of the legislature and elections. The chief
officer of the Council was neither an elected official nor a
member of the cabinet; the new Minister of Education was
both. This served to increase the visibility of the issues over
French schools, as the old system of conflict agents established
under the Council collapsed.

In 1883, a conference of representatives of the province's
Francophone groups was convened in Windsor. Although a list
of delegates was not available, it may be assumed that some
were from nearby Tecumseh. A resolution was passed requesting that the government give some attention to French
schools. Two years later, following an inquiry that showed
there were twenty-seven exclusively French schools in Ontario,
general instructions were sent to all teachers specifying the
amount of English that must be taught (Sissons 1917, p. 35).
Six years later, the teaching of French was prohibited in the
public schools (Brault 1966, p. 12). This prompted the
Tecumseh board to shift from a public to a separate school
status in order to preserve the use of French, a decision which
would later have considerable bearing on its financing.

Around the turn of the century, Franco-Ontarians held
several meetings pressing for additional resources for French
education and attempting to preserve their position in the

province. In 1906, two large-scale rallies were held: one in Walkerville, a few miles west of Tecumseh, and the other in Ottawa. These and other meetings led to the Congrès d'Education held in 1910. A total of 1245 representatives from Franco-Ontarian agencies attended. Of this group, seventy-two were from Essex county, sixteen of whom were from Tecumseh (A.C.F.E.0. 1910, p. 56). L'Association canadienne-française d'éducation d'Ontario, an outcome of the 1910 Congrès, forwarded a list of demands to the government, basing their appeal on the B.N.A. Act's reference to two official languages. The government refused their demands on the grounds that French-language schools would not be "organized upon a racial basis" but the religious basis stipulated at Confederation would be recognized (Walker 1964 pp. 246-247).

It was at this point that English Catholics allied with the English Protestant majority. Their rationalization was that to align with the French Catholics on the language issue would jeopardize the whole separate school system. As the English Catholics' opposition to French requests were put before the government mainly by their clergy, their conflict agencies were hardly involved at all. The clergy were generally strong in their opposition to bilingual schools. The attack was especially strong in Essex County and eventually spread beyond the question of bilingual schools to encompass the use of French in churches as well as in schools. The Bishop of the Diocese of London, in which Tecumseh was located led the attack against the French influence in schools and parishes.

By 1909, the major English Protestant conflict agency, the Orange Lodge, was increasing its activity against bilingual schools. This was in addition to the English press and spokespeople for the major Protestant denominations. At a general meeting in 1909, the Lodge decided "to investigate the state of Public Schools in Ontario, especially where bilingual schools exist" (Walker 1964, p. 235). Following the Franco-Ontarian Congrès d'Education, the Lodge called for the abolition of bilingual schools and, during the 1911 elections, attempted to obtain pledges from candidates assuring their opposition to bilingual schools (Walker 1964, pp. 254, 259).

Regulation 17. Instructions Number 17 or Regulation 17, issued in June, 1912, contained the following points:

1. A statement to the effect that there were only two classes of primary schools in Ontario — public and separate, but for convenience of reference, the term English-French was applied to schools in which French was the language of instruction.

2. Where necessary, French was permitted as the language of instruction and communication, but not beyond Form I [Grades 1 and 2].

3. Apart from the exception granted above, French would be permitted for only one hour a day in all. forms subject to the approval of parents and the supervising inspector.

4. A thorough system of inspection was provided for, and no teacher would be permitted to teach without proper knowledge of English. (Walker 1964, p. 267).

The immediate effect was a further de-institutionalization of the conflict. The regulation reduced the legitimacy that French-language schools had held up to 1885 by explicitly reducing the extent to which the language could be used as a medium of instruction. It explicitly stated that French schools would not be recognized as such; there would be only two classes of schools, public and separate. It also reduced the effectiveness of French inspectors as conflict agents.

During the next few years, the intensity of the conflict increased as Franco-Ontarians mobilized to oppose Regulation 17 and Anglophones countered their moves. At the opening of the 1912-13 school year, the Ottawa Separate School Board decided to resist the regulation. The resistance movement spread throughout the province. In the summer of 1916, the acting Minister of Education reported that 270 bilingual schools had "refused to follow Instructions 17 until compelled to do so" (Walker 1964, pp. 270, 289). The government compelled conformity by requiring teachers to sign a pledge committing themselves to obedience; withdrawing departmental grants from delinquent boards; and preventing locally collected taxes being used to pay the salaries of delinquent teachers (Walker 1964, p. 271). Teachers in the North Essex district, which included Tecumseh, considered noncompliance, but did not follow through. The more militant activity was limited to the Ottawa region.

In Windsor and Essex County the protest was closely tied to a related protest over the use of French in local parishes. The fact the Bishop sided with Anglophones on the school issue only served to tie the two issues together more strongly. Less than orderly demonstrations were reported in Windsor. One priest was dismissed and others were reprimanded for accusing their Bishop of having ordered that French not be used in local schools. In one parish, parishioners attempted to prevent a replacement priest entering their church and the Bishop was alleged to have called the police to restore order.[2] Although no violent demonstrations took place in Tecumseh, in 1915 a special meeting was held to protest the Bishop's position on both the church and school issues. It concluded with a petition expressing a lack of confidence in the Bishop.

Essex County was the scene for several meetings after Regulation 17 was issued. During the summer of 1912, members of local Orange Lodges met in Kingsville, some forty miles west of Tecumseh, to denounce bilingual schools and call for yet stronger regulations. Meetings and counter-meetings continued with some regularity until 1914. Several Francophone inspectors were dismissed for objecting to Regulation 17. This eliminated key conflict agents who, by their position, had served to maintain a certain amount of order between the parties.

Local involvement was most obvious in Tecumseh during the election of 1914, the first following Regulation 17. The campaign focused on North Essex, the Tecumseh constituency, where the seat had been held by a Franco-Ontarian cabinet minister in the Conservative Government responsible for the regulation. At the Conservative Party meeting in Tecumseh in

---

2. I have no direct documentation of these demonstrations. They are hinted at in the report of the clergy accused of improper behaviour by the Bishop (London, Province of Canada, Causes des Curés Dénoncés, 1914); and in an article written by Monique Chénier which appeared in *Le Droit*, Ottawa, May 30, 1966. Many references to these demonstrations were made by those interviewed in 1965 and 1966 in Tecumseh and Windsor. One respondent mentioned that his uncle had been among those arrested during the Windsor demonstrations.

June, 1914, a Francophone resident was nominated over the former member (Windsor, *The Evening Record*, June 5, 1914). Another Francophone had been nominated by the Liberals a few weeks earlier (Windsor, *The Evening Record*, June 1, 1914). The two opposed each other on platforms throughout the county; Regulation 17 was the central issue. The Liberals won the seat though the Conservative Government was returned to power with losses in those areas where there were significant proportions of Francophones (Walker 1964, p. 283).

A New Accommodation. Though Regulation 17 severely limited the use of French in Ontario schools, reduced the authority of Francophone inspectors, and refused to recognize the existence of French schools per se, it did not deny the legitimacy of the French party. The parties to the conflict were still intact and there remained a degree of mutual recognition. The regulation provided a statement of policy over which negotiations might take place, thereby beginning the process of returning the issue to the private level of the Department of Education bureaucracy.

To this effect an amendment to the regulation was introduced in 1913. The chief inspector, an administrative position, was given authority to extend the use of French beyond the first form, according to local circumstances (Walker 1964, pp. 280-281). This reintroduced an area for negotiation between local and provincial conflict agents. The entry of the Vatican into the dispute over the use of French in church services further contributed to increasing the level of institutionalization by recognizing the French party and its claims within the Catholic community (Walker 1964, pp. 302-308).

Further negotiations led to the appointment of yet another commission to inquire into the French-English schools in 1925. In contrast with previous commissions, this one consisted of three members representing the contending parties: a French Catholic, a member of the Department of Education, and an English Protestant (Walker 1964, p. 314).

The commission's report did not request a repeal of the regulation, but recommended that French and English directors of education be appointed to deal with local school boards and assist with decisions on the extent to which French could be used in any given school district. The commission's report, accepted in 1927, was received by most Franco-Ontarians with satisfaction. The bilingual schools immediately moved to reorganize under a set of modified regulations. The Tecumseh Separate School Board passed a motion establishing the "system of parallel classes as suggested in the...investigation committee's report and recommended [by the inspector]" (Tecumseh Separate School Board, January 28, 1928). The local newspaper noted some three years later that

> the new system in force for only a few years has already proved itself in spite of numerous difficulties inherited from the period of transition. The results from all points of view are very satisfying. (Tecumseh, *La Feuille d'Erable*, April 16, 1931)

The new accommodation provided a temporary return to tranquility in the school situation. During the thirties and into the forties, the major issue occupying the Tecumseh Separate School Board was that of finances, a problem shared by all Catholic schools.

The Pressure of the Sixties. The system of conflict agents evolving from the accommodation of 1927 managed to keep the issues of French-language instruction fairly well contained within the bureaucratic structures up to the early sixties. For the most part, issues were dealt with administratively in two ways. First, various Francophone conflict agencies, such as the A.P.I. and the S.S.J.B., articulated interests from local to extra-local levels and back again through their regional and provincial bodies. Second, the dual inspectorate and the custom of French and English principals and vice-principals, combined with French and English teachers groups, provided the means to deal with most issues arising at the local level.

However, although Tecumseh remained overwhelmingly Catholic in population, until the early fifties it was predominantly French Catholic in character. In 1941 almost three-quarters of the town's population was of French origin; by 1951 this had dropped to 63.3 percent. In 1957, pupils enrolled in the French panel were still in a majority, slim though that majority may have been. The potential for an increase in issues within parish and school and the testing of the effectiveness of the conflict-agent system began in the mid-fifties as the Anglophone population in the town showed signs of rapidly increasing. These signs are quite apparent in the school enrolment figures presented in Figure 6.

It was at this point, in 1957, when the Anglophone population was on the increase and contacts over language use were becoming more frequent in parish and school, that Francophone members of the Catholic Parent-Teacher Association separated to form their own L'Association de Parents et d'Instituteurs. A statement was made by the Anglophone president of the C.P.T.A. at the meeting when this separation was announced. The following excerpt from that statement reveals some of the issues involved.

> For those of us who are not aware of the problem, I might point out that when the P.T.A. was first organized in the parish, it was decided that the business meeting should be *conducted in English*, and that the French language be considered *only as one phase* of our interests. On several occasions since that time, the pros and cons of forming a separate organization to handle the problems of the French classes have been discussed at length, and each time it was apparently found unfeasible. However, there is still a group who are convinced that this is a necessary organization, and it is this faction that's proceeding with the organization of the A.P.I. as a separate organization. (Italics added)

A new conflict agency was born, forming an additional link between local, regional and provincial agencies.

Agencies such as the A.P.I. worked through local conflict agents when issues of the type which could be settled locally arose. A look at a few such issues will provide some insight into the dynamics of the conflict-agent system. In the autumn of 1965 complaints were heard in A.P.I. meetings about the teaching of health and physical education. French was not being used and the amount scheduled was more than that prescribed for the French panel. The complaint was referred to the board and on October 1965, the French and English inspectors were invited to discuss the matter. The English inspector was very careful to restrict his statements to the prescribed requirements for the English panel. The French inspector noted that for "his side," the amount of P.T.A instruction exceeded the requirements and promised to investigate. An inspection was carried out within a week or two. The head of the French panel was instructed to see that the time be reduced and that health classes be taught in French.

Another issue arising at the beginning of the school year in 1965 involved only the Anglophone principal of Ste-Anne's intermediate School and the French inspector. There were approximately twenty-two pupils in the English panel grade ten, and nine in the French panel. According to the principal, it was impossible to operate two grade tens with such low enrolments. He therefore wanted to combine the two panels in one classroom. This required consultation with the other party since the French panel was involved.

His first move was to check with the English inspector, who approved the proposed move. He then contacted the French inspector who turned the question back to him for his suggestion:

> I think he first felt me out — for my reasons — to make sure that I wasn't out to smother the bilingual classes. I assured him that they would be guaranteed their seven periods of "le français" a week.

The French inspector reported that:

> The principal asked me to make a suggestion. I had no choice. So they were separated only for special French. This is a problem in high schools today, with options and different courses, you can't maintain a small class or two grades in one room. I didn't approve, but to object wasn't practical.

The presence of an effective system of decision making that recognizes both parties and their claims was probably re-

sponsible for preventing a magnification of these kinds of issues. Both were managed smoothly and quickly at the administrative level, with little public visibility. Conflict agents,
through their status and role-sets, tied the local level to the
Department of Education on one hand, and to conflict agencies
on the other.

The linguistic claims of the French party, as distinct
from the religious claims they shared with Anglophone
Catholics, had perhaps received a greater degree of recognition
by the early sixties. Since 1927 various administrative
concessions had been made, the consequences of which were a
further recognition of the legitimacy of the French party. For
example, the Department of Education, in lieu of recognizing
bilingual secondary schools as such, granted permission for
additional subjects to be taught in French. Furthermore, the
number of potential conflict-agent positions in the system had
increased considerably.

By 1965, the degree to which the relations between
Anglophones and Francophones in Tecumseh, and in Ontario
in general, were institutionalized was relatively high.
However, the demand for official legislative recognition of
French or bilingual schools from kindergarten to university
remained unmet. The bilingual schools were defined simply as
"schools attended by French-speaking pupils." Thus, the policy
stated in Regulation 17 that there were only two classes of
schools — public and separate — remained intact.

One cannot underestimate the effects of the "quiet revolution" in Quebec on French-English relations in Ontario. The
"maître chez nous" slogan of the years of the Lesage
Government and the increasing clarity with which new separatist organizations articulated that option for Quebec had two
outcomes which influenced attitudes and behaviour in Ontario.
First, Franco-Ontarians experienced a new pride in identity,
given the forward and aggressive push of Quebec. Secondly,
Anglophones in Ontario acquired a new, though limited, sen-
sitivity to the demands of Franco-Ontarians. Bilingualism,
perhaps a century too late, had acquired a respectability and
was proposed by some as the solution to Canadian unity.

The federal government created the Royal Commission
on Bilingualism and Biculturalism in 1963. The Commission

held hearings across Canada during 1964. Tecumseh agencies and citizens attended and presented briefs at the hearings held in Windsor on April 30, 1964. A preliminary report was published in 1965, the report on education in 1968. The same year, the Official Languages Act was passed enacting legislation arising from the Commission's recommendations. The focus was on Confederation, Canadian unity, and bilingualism. These events provided an opportunity for reopening to the public the issues surrounding French schools in Ontario. In its brief to the Commission, the A.C.F.E.O. based its claims on the British North America Act, noting that:

> for all practical purposes Confederation was a pact arrived at between the people of English Canada and French Canada through the mediation of their representatives.
> (A.C.F.E.O., Mémoire à la Commission, 1964, p.17)

The brief went on to note that:

> too often, unfortunately, persons are inclined to believe, especially outside of Quebec, that the shelving of Regulation 17 brought a solution to all the problems of the French Canadians living in Ontario.
> (A.C.F.E.O. Mémoire à la Commission, 1964, p. 12)

The Ontario Government responded positively. Legislation passed in the summer of 1968 finally recognized the existence of French-language schools, a claim first articulated by Franco-Ontarians in the 1880's. The Secondary Schools and Boards of Education Amendment Act, 1968 permitted boards to "establish and maintain secondary schools or classes in secondary schools for the purpose of providing for the use of the French language in instruction..." (Article 10, Section 113). The Schools Administration Amendment Act, 1968 provided the same opportunity for elementary boards, both public and separate (Article 9, Section 35d). Both Acts specified numbers of ratepayers, pupils, and/or parents required in order to compel a board to provide French-language classes in English schools, but left the decisions regarding

170

French-language schools to the local boards. This fact, whether by oversight or intent, opened the door to fairly intense local conflicts.

In addition, the Act, in referring to secondary schools, provided for the creation of French-language advisory committees to local boards. These were to be composed of three members appointed by a board and four French-speaking ratepayers selected by Francophone ratepayers in the school district (Article 10, Section 114). This move added a new conflict agency to the system, one which was legally recognized and could articulate local interests at the local level.

There were few problems at the elementary school level; most of the contact took place in separate schools where conflict-agent systems were well established. Nor were there many problems over the establishment and extension of French-language classes. However, at the secondary school level, Francophones were for the first time coming into contact with English Protestants rather than Catholics. New systems had to be established; but the process was less than harmonious. The issues focused on the establishment of French-language schools. This would involve moving both French and English pupils around, and building new schools. Such moves were bound to bring the question of French schools back into public view.

In Toronto, a few months after the legislation was passed the Metropolitan School Commission rejected the principle of creating separate schools for French pupils in favour of creating French panels in existing schools (*Le Devoir*, Montreal, December 19, 1968). A French-language school was eventually established in the Toronto region a year later (*Le Devoir*, Montreal, August 26, 1969). A much more intense struggle occurred in the west end of Ottawa in 1970 where English conflict agencies attempted to block the creation of such a school in their district (*Le Devoir*, Montreal, February 7, 1970). An injunction, dismissed by the court, was applied for in order to prevent the school being established. These are but examples of local conflicts that indicated an increased intensity in the relationships as a result of the new legislation.

The two most notable confrontations took place in Sturgeon Falls in 1971 and Cornwall in 1973. Both of these involved massive demonstrations and student strikes. Both required the appointment of special mediators by the Department of Education. The Sturgeon Falls confrontation arose out of the refusal of the Nipissing Regional School Commission to create a French-language secondary school, in spite of the fact that the ratio was 1,321 Francophone to 365 Anglophone students.

The affair in Sturgeon Falls led to the appointment of the Ministerial Commission on French-Language Secondary Education. The report of this Commission, submitted in 1972, recommended that the authority of French-language advisory committees be strengthened, a committee on linguistic rights be established to act as a higher-level appeal device in local disputes over language, and a standing committee, headed by an assistant deputy minister, be appointed within the Department of Education to deal with French-language schools. This latter recommendation was immediately adopted, with a Francophone assistant deputy minister appointed as chairman.

Before the government was able to act on the other recommendations of the report, a confrontation broke out in Cornwall following bitter but brief confrontations between the regional board and its French-language advisory committee (*Le Droit*, Ottawa, March 14, 1973). A dispute over establishing a French language secondary school led to a strike of French-language students with parent and teacher support. The strike drew considerable support from Francophone groups throughout the Ottawa Valley counties. After the immediate issues were settled, the board suspended two Francophone teachers for their alleged leadership in the strike. This led to further escalation until a settlement was reached early in 1974.

During the autumn of 1973, the Ontario Legislature finally passed two acts, referred to as Bills 180 and 181, which implemented the major recommendations of the 1972 Ministerial Commission Report. Bill 180 strengthened the French-language advisory committees. Bill 181 called on the Minister of Education to set up a Commission of Languages of Instruction composed of five members, two of whom must be Francophones and two Anglophones. The Commission would act as an appeal body in disputes such as those in Sturgeon Falls and Cornwall. These two Acts, combined with the earlier legislation and the new Standing Committee on French-Language Schools, once again served to return the dispute to the Department of Education and related bodies. However, the question of establishing French-language schools was left in the hands of local boards, although under some control and with the possibility of appeal.

The 1968 legislation stimulated considerable activity in Essex County. There were French classes in some of the secondary schools in the county and in Windsor, but no composite French-language school. Franco-Ontarians had long been dissatisfied with French classes in predominantly English schools. With an overwhelming majority of English-speaking students and teachers, the atmosphere of these schools was decidedly Anglophone. Assemblies, announcements and school services such as guidance were all in English. French was really only a concession, a relatively unimportant addition to the main stream. This problem was recognized and its amelioration sanctioned by the 1972 Ministerial Commission Report:

> For the French-speaking community, the key element in a French language school is that the language of communication and of administration, and hence the total ambiance of the school, should be French....What nearly always happens in...mixed schools is that the language of communication and administration, and thus the overall atmosphere, proves to be English. Much more often than not, the mixed or so-called "bilingual school" is a one-way street to assimilation for the French-speaking student.
> (Ministerial Commission 1972, pp. 14-15)

Given the number of children of high school age from French-speaking families in the county and Windsor, Franco-Ontarians were quick to move in accordance with the 1968 legislation. In January 1969, the Essex County Board received letters from the regional body of L'Association canadienne-française de l'Ontario requesting consideration for a French-language high school in the district (*The Windsor Star*, January 23, 1969). By early February of that year, the French-language advisory committees to the city and county boards had been elected. A Tecumseh resident was a member of the county advisory committee. In March, 800 people attended a meeting held in Tecumseh to discuss the possibilities of establishing a French-language school in the region (*The Windsor Star*, March 3, 1969).

As in other parts of Ontario, this was the first experience with public school boards over the language of instruction issue. Previously, most confrontations had taken place within the confines of the Catholic community. Now that high schools were involved, Francophones found themselves more closely tied to Protestant or non-Catholic interests. There was a subtle resistance to the notion of a French-language high school by both city and county boards, though the county board was more responsive. Needless to say, French-speaking communities in the county were far more obvious and stronger than in the city.

The reality of a French-speaking community seemed to come as a surprise to many Anglophones not associated with Catholic institutions. This was apparent in interviews conducted in 1965-66. Protestant Anglophones in Windsor, not in Tecumseh, expressed surprise at research being conducted on French-English relations in their region. A typical reply was: "There are a lot of Italians here, but I don't think there are many French. There used to be years ago, but they've all assimilated." Members of both city and county boards, therefore, met their French language advisory committees in 1969 in a state of perplexity.

It was with some reluctance that the city of Windsor board granted honoraria, required by the legislation, to members of the advisory committee. Three trustees attempted to delay payment, one expressed worry about the committee's recommendations, and the board refused to consider membership in the Bilingual School Trustees' Association (*The Windsor Star*, March 27, 1969). Some members of the Essex County Board expressed opposition to the busing of French-speaking students in the county to French classes held at the

Belle River district high school. One suggested that such a move amounted to segregation, pointing out that in the United States schools were never equal when separate (*The Windsor Star*, March 10, 1970). It was in this atmosphere that the French-language advisory committees and the regional L'Association canadienne-française de l'Ontario had to push for a French-language secondary school.

The debate continued to the end of 1973 without a final solution. Francophone representatives were pushing for a single school which required the two boards to share in financing and administration. This in itself, though extremely reasonable, caused delay. Several questionnaires were sent out to parents to determine the numbers of pupils available and how much support the school would have. None were conclusive. Questionnaires, if used by inexperienced people, only cause further delay, even if it is not intentional. Furthermore, interpretation of results without necessary tests of reliability and validity may lead to erroneous conclusions. Early in 1973, the two French-language committees presented a final report or brief to both boards. The report indicated an adequate student body and suggested that the school should be located "in the general vicinity of the Town of Tecumseh" (Brief 1972, pp. 6-8). The boards accepted the recommendations in principle. A committee of four was created to investigate further, but only one of the four appointed to the committee was a Francophone (*The Windsor Star*, April 26, 1973; *Le Droit*, Ottawa, September 15, 1973).

Elementary schooling in French, however, related Francophones to a different structure. Beginning in 1969, separate schools in Tecumseh — the only schools containing French panels — related to the Essex County Roman Catholic Separate School Board. This board was responsible for Catholic education up to and including grade ten. In January, 1969, twenty-three local boards, including the Tecumseh Separate School Board, were consolidated under a county board. There was some resistance to this move on the part of local Francophones because they feared being dominated by the Anglophone sectors of the county. According to the county board administrator: "This resistance died when it became apparent that the new board was favourable to Francophone

175

schools." The extent of this favourability will not be tested until local Francophones formally ask for a composite French-language elementary school to be established in Tecumseh.

Though consolidation resulted in a better distribution of resources for education throughout the county, leading to capital improvements in Tecumseh and elsewhere, the fundamental problem of financing Catholic education remained paramount. The discussions which began in 1966 over a complete sharing of facilities between Ste-Anne's Intermediate School and the parochial high school continued into 1973. As far as French education is concerned, the system of conflict agents, with minor modification, remained intact following consolidation. Issues which did arise were handled as they were in 1966. What had changed was that, with the ever-increasing proportion of Anglophone students in Tecumseh's St-Antoine's School, the atmosphere of the school had become decidedly English. Such was not the case eight years previously.

The board had made successful attempts at shifting French panel students from nearby points in the county into St-Antoine's to strengthen the French program, and the board's assistant superintendent responsible for French education had plans to ameliorate this situation further. Two related issues were on the horizon at the time of writing. One had to do with the distribution of monies designated for French education. Classrooms where French is the language of instruction is one thing, but without basic back-up services in French, such as libraries, film libraries, guidance, and adequate substitute teachers, the French language becomes but a symbol of Anglophone tolerance. A request for a change in the distribution of funds will increase the visibility of the French programs.[3]

---

3. The issue of funds available for French programs was related to a decision on the part of Ontario to use a different formula for distributing funds designated for bilingual education. With respect to Ontario, the federal authority recommended that 9 percent of the grants be allocated to Francophones receiving their education in French and 5 percent to Anglophones studying French. Ontario, acting within its jurisdiction, decided to alocate the grants on an equal basis to both groups, thus cutting off potential funds for French education in the province (*Le Droit*, Ottawa, April 27, 1973; June 16, 1973).

The Conflict System

The move to create a French-language elementary school within the county, possibly using St-Antoine's in Tecumseh, will undoubtedly bring opposition and perhaps delaying tactics similar to those used by the public school boards over the secondary school issue. Already in the spring of 1973, even though no formal proposals had been made, some board members expressed concern over the way in which school facilities might be redistributed should one school be "turned over to the French." The fact remains that if steps are not taken to ameliorate French schooling in the county's separate school system beyond what has already been done, there is a definite possibility of further disintegration.

This concludes the analysis of the conflict system in Catholic and French education in Tecumseh. Underlying the analysis is a set of concepts and the implied relations between these concepts. I have, for example, referred to the institutionalization of conflict relations and implied an association between institutionalization and the intensity exhibited by a conflict. These concepts and their relations will now be made explicit.

Chapter Seven

A Paradigm for the Analysis
of Community Conflict

At the beginning of this study I noted that experience is organized through selecting those aspects of reality that have meaning within a cultural heritage, personal history, social position, and objectives of the moment. The essential difference between the scientist and the layman is that the former proceeds in a much more systematic fashion. His or her objectives are research problems, propositions and hypotheses derived from the theoretical orientations of a discipline. The selective devices are concepts defined as precisely as possible. In the course of dealing with experience or data, new concepts may be required and old ones may be refined or discarded. These in turn become a part of the theoretical orientations of the discipline.

The concepts, their interrelations, and the investigative and analytical procedures used in a research endeavour together present a paradigm. It was in this sense that Robert K. Merton referred to "analytical paradigms" as models or patterns containing the "array of assumptions, concepts and basic propositions employed in a sociological analysis" (Merton 1957, p. 13). Up to this point, the paradigm used in this study has not been clearly articulated, though I have presented the basic orientations and, when appropriate, introduced certain key concepts and their interrelations. The task of this chapter is to present the paradigm. By proceeding in this manner, I am being more faithful to the research process as it took place than if I had introduced at the beginning a set of hypotheses for an empirical test. The paradigm which we will now examine developed out of the interaction between those events observed and the ideas that I and others had about assimilation, conflict, linguistic and ethnic groups, and so on. That is, the paradigm was a result of an interaction between data and theory, an interaction sustained throughout the entire process.

General Orientations

This was a community study and, as such, a basic assumption
was made about the significance of locality-based relationships,
both for individual citizens and, from a sociological point of
view, for an adequate understanding of current social behaviour in Canada. I am reminded of a statement by John R.
Seeley and others made in *Crestwood Heights*. Crestwood
Heights

> exists as *a community* because of the relationships
> that exist between people — relationships revealed
> in the functioning of the institutions which they
> have created: family, school, church, community
> centre, club, association, summer camp, and other
> more peripheral institutions and services.
> (Seeley, et al. 1956, pp. 3-4)

So it was with Tecumseh. French Catholic, English Catholic
and English Protestant related to each other through a set of
institutions and organizations created by them. The relationship between the local or community and extra-local systems
was taken into account, acknowledging the very great extent to
which extra-local systems impinge on local communities.
   Nevertheless, the stated significance of locality remained
an assumption that was not tested in this research. There was
also a value component tied to this assumption — the belief on
my part that locality-based relationships are an important and
desirable aspect of the human condition. Opportunities for a
greater breadth and depth of participation are more likely to
occur either in city neighbourhoods or in towns and villages.
These opportunities are dependent upon the continued existence of local decision-making mechanisms. Of course, such
decisions must significantly affect the lives of local residents
according to their definition of the situation. Otherwise, local
participation is but "as sounding brass, or a tinkling cymbal."
   A social realist orientation may be added to the
paradigm. In this study, I took the position that members of
social categories or collectivities are "bound together in a

system of mutual influences which has sufficient character to be described as a process" (Park and Burgess, 1921, p. 36). The very concepts, *social category* and *collectivity*, emerged from this orientation. Though I trust that I did not reify these concepts, the orientation nevertheless led to the decision to focus on social conflict rather than assimilation.

It is difficult to recall whether the social realist orientation developed in the course of early observations in the field or whether it was present in my mind to begin with. In any case, I did begin this work with assimilation as a key concept, only later shifting to conflict relations. The literature on assimilation directs one toward indicators which are attributes of individuals. In studies of French-English relations, language is a typical example. The indicator, mother tongue or language used at home or some other variation, is measured for each individual and then added giving an aggregate measure which is taken to represent the degree of assimilation of a group. This operation yields only a partial picture. It tells us little about the way in which people who identify with and are identified as members of social categories or collectivities interact with others in terms of such identities.

Early observations in the field led me away from a concentration on individual attributes. What I saw and heard were people dealing with each other in schools, churches, voluntary associations and town halls on the basis of being identified as French or English, Protestant or Catholic. Interaction took place in terms of perceived and real collective interests and threats to those interests. Of more importance, the same people did not behave in the same way with each other on all occasions. Given certain issues or events, membership in one or another category would be brought into play. Each individual occupies a multiplicity of roles and seldom if ever acts out all simultaneously. To be French or English in Tecumseh is a social role. That role is activated given certain conditions. Depending on a person's location in other systems, for example, social class, or occupational status, and the presence of certain events, such as issues regarding language of instruction in secondary schools, the role will be revived or remain dormant. The fact that it remains dormant does not mean that the individual is assimilated nor that the collective

representations emerging from the history of his or her group
have disappeared.

These observations led to social conflict as a more adequate perspective for dealing with interaction among people
insofar as that interaction was based upon their membership in
linguistically based categories. The kinds of issues and events
which appeared to activate roles related to language and
religion were those which had to do with collective interests
and threats to those interests. It was in this sense that I
stated earlier that conflict over language would be viewed not
as the result of disgruntled malcontents, but as a consequence
of membership in particular social categories. Not all relationships between people and groups are conflict relations. For
this reason, it was necessary to specify those conditions which,
when observed, would indicate the presence of a conflict situation. The conditions required for a state of conflict to exist
were posited as follows:

1. two or more parties exhibiting a level of organization
   beyond that of simple aggregates or statistical
   categories;
2. two or more parties who must be in contact with each
   other;
3. a state of resource scarcity and/or value incompatibility.

A problem to which the literature on social conflict is frequently addressed is that of differentiating between conflict
and other forms of interaction, especially between conflict and
competition. Park and Burgess used contact between
individuals or groups as a key characteristic.

> Competition takes the form of conflict or rivalry
> only when it becomes conscious, when competitors
> identify one another as rivals or as ene-
> mies....Competition is a struggle between
> individuals who are not necessarily in contact and
> communication; while conflict is a contest in which
> contact is an indispensible condition.
> (Park and Burgess 1921, pp. 507, 574)

Robin Williams Jr., in a recent consideration of the problem, defines pure competition as a situation in which each party is striving for the same object at the same time. In contrast, in pure conflict, each party's objective is to annihilate, defeat, or subjugate the other (Williams 1970, p. 218). This is acceptable, to a point. However, it permits Professor Williams to exclude incompatibilities open to negotiation, compromise and settlement from being considered as conflict. There is the common tendency to view conflict only in terms of its violent manifestations. The discussion by Park and Burgess does not lead in this direction. Elections "in which we count noses when we do not break heads" are also taken as a form of conflict (Park and Burgess 1921, p. 575).

The perspective implied in Williams' discussion does not permit one to deal with institutionalized conflicts that show considerable continuity. It stresses, rather, the settlement of issues which, though catalysts, are but symbols of continuing states of conflict. "Conflict may assume the form of civil war, or of parliamentary debate, of a strike, or of a well-regulated negotiation" (Dahrendorf 1959, p. 135). It is better to take the extent to which a conflict is regulated, the intensity of a conflict, and the degree of violence as variables of conflict situations rather than to posit various levels attained by these variables as different types of conflicts or different types of social relations.

By adopting this orientation, one would tend not to view every new manifestation of a continuing conflict with surprise, or attempt to deal with it as an isolated event which, once settled, suggests that the conflict is over. Such has been the position of many Anglophones each time a school issue has arisen in one or another province. Since a similar issue was settled in 1867, or 1927, or some other date, it was assumed that the conflict itself had been settled. The perspective adopted here assumed that while the above conditions are met, a state of conflict exists.

Before considering the conceptual framework, another value component of the paradigm merits attention. I have adopted a position on French-English relations which holds that pluralism is a desirable arrangement. Another way of stating the same thing is to say that I do not favour assimilation. There is, I believe, a consistency between this value and that concerning locality-based relationships. The stress is on the quest for community at one level and heterogeneity at the national level. Nevertheless, the processes of industrialization and bureaucratization erode differences, and tend to encourage uniformity. The present resurgence of ethnic and national identities is most likely a counter-movement.

In taking this position, I am likely to find myself in conflict with another position to which I adhere. Empirically, exploitation usually accompanies pluralism. This impedes equality. I am inclined to think that it is not possible to have a pluralism of national identity while at the same time maintaining an equality of opportunity. It is this inclination that argues strongly in favour of the secession of Quebec.

The Conceptual Framework

A significant portion of this study was devoted to establishing the existence and characteristics of the three parties to the conflict under consideration. The marshalling of evidence, historical and contemporary, about the forces of association and dissociation in Tecumseh was for the sole purpose of determining the presence of social categories or collectivities based on linguistic and religious affiliations. Two major sets of criteria were used; the objective criteria of observed interaction and the subjective criteria of definition of membership by self and others.

It was then necessary to establish the fact of interaction among the parties *qua* parties. The introduction of the concepts of conflict agencies and agents as the links contributed to an understanding of the way in which the parties interacted. The final task was to note the existence of resource scarcity and incompatible values of the parties.

This whole exercise also provided a framework for describing the people and institutions of Tecumseh, though admittedly the description was limited by the particular focus of the study. Nevertheless, we did get a picture of the life of the town through two primary organizational dimensions, language and religion. Once the required conditions were demonstrated, two general questions were posited. The first was about the way in which conflicts vary according to involvement and commitment of party members, and according to the types of action taken. If variations of this type could be demonstrated, then the next question would direct our attention toward those factors that conditioned the variations.

Variations in Conflict Intensity

Certainly conflicts vary in strength or force. The problem for the researcher is to specify what events permit judgements about the relative strength of a given conflict. That is, what are suitable indicators of this type of variation.

Early observations in the field suggested that the strength of a conflict varies along at least two dimensions which, though closely related, show some degree of independence. Several hours in Tecumseh were spent attending meetings and conferences devoted to the articulation of Franco-Ontarian interests. The numbers of people involved and the frequency of such meetings suggested a variation in the extent to which party members were involved. At the same time, these sessions were quite calm; there were no threatening or intimidating statements directed at opponents; few press releases were made; and there were no efforts to circulate petitions or organize demonstrations. In other words, members of one of the conflict parties appeared to be fairly extensively involved. However, in terms of tactics used, the actions of the participants were extremely passive. These observations suggest two variables to describe the strength of a conflict, *intensity and militancy.*[1]

The intensity of a conflict refers to the size of party involvement. If all the members of social categories or collectivities in conflict were participants through conflict agencies, the level of intensity would be at a maximum. We may assume

----

1. This distinction is based on Dahrendorf's conceptualization of intensity and violence which appeared unsatisfactory for the data under study. His notion of violence, for example, included all "manifestations" of conflict from peaceful discussion to the actual use of force. I preferred to use the more general category of militancy to include the range of actions, from passive to violent (Dahrendorf, 1959, pp.212-213).

that this maximum level is seldom reached, but the degree of
intensity does appear to vary according to certain other conditions. These will be discussed later. In contrast, militancy
refers to the nature of specific acts directed against the opponent rather than the extent to which people are involved in
these acts. Militancy is the use of compelling or coercive measures in the pursuit of party interests.

Certainly, the two variables are closely related. A certain
degree of intensity would appear to be a prerequisite for militant behaviour. All other things remaining equal, militancy
usually elicits a response in kind and may, therefore, increase
the level of intensity. Referring to Table 28, cells one, two, and
four are empirically possible. The state suggested in cell three
is assumed to be empirically rare. Cells one and four correspond to the commonly made distinction between overt and
covert conflict. In some cases, conflict per se is defined in
terms of cell one and cell four is referred to as potential or
latent conflict. We might now look at Chapter 6 in the light of
the varying conditions represented in Table 28.

Table 28
Relationship Between Militancy and Intensity

1. Intensity High Militancy High	2. Intensity High MilitancyLow
3. Intensity Low Militancy High	4. Intensity Low Militancy Low

The first task is to specify the indicators used. The following items were taken as components of intensity: (1) the
emergence of conflict agencies; (2) the extent to which agencies
pursued the interests of their parties; and (3) the viability of
the agencies themselves. The observed appearance of new
agencies and the quantity of agency activity in interest
aggregation and articulation were the indicators of the first

two components. The size of agency memberships and the level of participation (attendance) were the indicators of viability.

The components of militancy were: (1) the use of compelling or intimidating actions in the pursuit of party interests; and (2) the use of coercive or violent actions in the pursuit of party interests. An observed use of force to injure or harm the opponent was taken as an indicator of coercion or violence. The use of petitions, demonstrations, and non-compliance were the indicators of compelling or intimidating acts.

A decision was made to focus on issues related to education and, though this has been a very significant battleground for the contending parties, other spheres of activity have also generated issues in French-English and Catholic-Protestant conflict. The basis from which Catholic schools operated was established in Ontario in 1863. From Confederation to 1900, issues pertaining to Catholic schools were dealt with administratively. By the turn of the century, it was noted that conditions in the society as a whole were beginning to place an increasing premium on education. Catholics were bound to press for an extension of previous agreements. The granting of continuation classes by the Department of Education raised the visibility of the issue itself. Pressure from Protestant groups prompted the Minister to act against the way in which Catholics were using the new regulation. In summary, between 1867 and 1900 both the intensity and militancy of the Catholic-Protestant conflict were at a low level, corresponding to cell four in Table 28. The intensity showed signs of increasing as Protestant agencies started to move against Catholic school privileges.

Between 1900 and 1940, indicators of increasing intensity became more apparent. In 1931, a new conflict agency, the Catholic Taxpayers' Association of Ontario, was formed drawing the laity into the struggle. Activity in Tecumseh increased as Francophone agencies joined with the C.T.A.O. Petitions were circulated throughout the province and in Tecumseh during the early thirties. Counter petitions were put out by Protestant agencies. Catholic schools were an important issue in the 1934 elections with both parties heavily involved. During this period, the situation corresponded to cell two in Table 28; intensity was relatively high and there were indications of a relatively low level of militancy. By the early forties, the situation had again returned to a state of low intensity with little manifestation, if any, of militant activity.

By the mid-fifties and into the sixties, several external factors contributed to increasing problems over financing Catholic education under existing arrangements and the issue became more visible. The Catholic Parent-Teacher Association in Tecumseh and its Francophone counterpart were becoming more and more involved with these problems. A new agency, the Tecumseh Catholic Education Association, entered the picture during the mid-sixties. Meetings were held throughout the region, student picketing was reported in Tecumseh and mass rallies were held in Toronto attended by Tecumseh students. Again, the pressure reached a peak during provincial elections. In 1971, Tecumseh residents were heavily involved in the election on behalf of Catholic interests. This period most certainly exhibited a relatively high level of intensity, and militant behaviour seemed to be running at a higher level than during the thirties.

The conflict over French schooling followed a similar pattern to the Catholic school issue. In Ontario, at the time of Confederation, schools in which French was the language of instruction were fairly well established. However, in contrast with Catholic education, the British North America Act left decisions on language of instruction to the provinces. The same conditions which had opened Catholic education to public view also affected French education. Education itself was becoming increasingly important. Ironically, the Francophones' desire to improve their school system led to an increasing visibility of the schools themselves and the beginning of several ministerial inquiries.

From this point on, we saw that events leading up to and following Regulation 17 showed increasing levels of intensity and militancy, the latter appearing to reach a higher level than in the case of Catholic education. Between 1900 and 1912, mass meetings and petitions, counter meetings and petitions, were common in and around Tecumseh. The formation of the A.C.F.E.O. in 1910 consolidated Francophone interests. English Catholics allied with English Protestants as French Catholics had allied with English Catholics in the thirties, further increasing involvement and extending the conflict into church and parish. Strong attacks on the use of French in both spheres of institutional activity were mounted in Essex County.

Regulation 17 reduced the recognition which French schools had held up to Confederation. Under the leadership of the A.C.F.E.0. and groups of teachers and school trustees, Francophones mobilized against the regulation. The strategies employed — non-compliance, petitions, and demonstrations — indicated an increasing level of militancy based on wide-spread involvement. Tecumseh was a focal point in the 1914 elections when local Conservatives refused to nominate an incumbent cabinet minister. Some concessions on the part of the government in 1927 started the process of returning the issue to negotiation.

During the thirties, the resources of both French and English Catholics were concentrated on the Catholic school issue. As far as French schooling was concerned, a system of conflict agents evolved as a means of managing local issues. The conflict had moved from a situation best represented by cell one in Table 28 to cell four. The level of intensity started to climb again during the late fifties. The first indicator in Tecumseh was the formation of the Association de Parents et d'Instituteurs as Francophones moved out of the predominantly Anglophone Catholic Parent-Teacher Association. There was a severe and obvious threat to French education in Tecumseh as the proportion of Anglophones in the population rapidly increased.

It was not until the mid-sixties, when pressure on secondary schools brought Francophones into direct contact with public school boards, that the situation began to move from the state represented in cell four to cell two. There was very little if any militant activity in Tecumseh as compared with that in Cornwall and Sturgeon Falls, for example. However, the intensity did increase as the regional A.C.F.E.0. and the new French-language advisory committees pressed for a French secondary school in Tecumseh.

This summary has highlighted the manner in which conflicts vary in strength according to the level of intensity and militancy shown at any given time as members of one or another party mobilize through conflict agencies to meet particular issues. It was impossible, however, to discuss these variations without referring to other factors which interacted with them.

Factors Influencing the Intensity and Militancy of Conflicts

I have frequently referred to factors external to, but influencing, the system under study. If we take the three parties as identified, their interaction, and relevant issues as a system, then external factors are those which are not directly a part of that system. The fact that values and practices concerning education rapidly changed at the turn of the century was not in itself a manifestation of French-English or Protestant-Catholic relations. However, these new values and practices, as was noted in Chapter 6, did influence the relationship between these social categories. If one assumed the *fact* of Catholic and/or French education and also those value orientations which translate the fact into a *right*, then requests by Catholics and Francophones for an extension and improvement of their school systems simply followed from those changes in education in general. However, requests of this type served to raise the public visibility of the fact so that the issue could be and was perceived as a threat to the majority's concept of its place in the scheme of things.

One must not underestimate the importance of visibility. As I have stated many times before, social conflicts are manifested through specific issues. Issues are solved or settled but, to the extent that the parties remain intact and the conditions for conflict remain unsettled, the conflict itself is not resolved. People are inclined to assume that when an issue has been settled, the conflict has been resolved. What has happened is that in settling the issue, methods which permit the parties to deal with each other have evolved. French-language advisory committees have been established, or "continuation classes" permitted, or French and English inspectors appointed, but these mechanisms for regulating conflict only reduce the visibility of the parties and their demands. The opposition is once more satisfied only to rise in a state of indignation when they discover anew, as a new issue surfaces, that the parties and their demands are still intact.

A Paradigm for the Analysis

The operative variable in this discussion in *institutionalization*. The extent to which conflicts are regulated is a common theme in the literature. Through regulatory devices some "conflicts [are] programmed for continuation" (Horowitz 1963, p. 183). Robert Dubin, in an analysis of industrial conflict, suggested that institutionalization is an inevitable outcome of continuous conflict situations (Dubin 1957, p. 187). To Ralf Dahrendorf, "conflict regulation" is "in many ways [a] most crucial factor affecting the empirical patterns of class conflict" (Dahrendorf 1959, p. 223).

An institutionalized conflict is one in which a set of regulations (rules or norms) and a set of positions and roles emerge to define and stabilize the relationship between the contenders, permitting each to interact with its opponent with some predictability. Accepting the statement that "institutionalization...is clearly a matter of degree," it follows that some conflicts may be more institutionalized than others or, over a period of time, any one conflict may show variations in institutionalization (Parsons 1951, p. 39). It is in this sense that institutionalization is viewed as a variable.

Labour-management relations provide a ready example of institutionalized conflict. Both parties are recognized; their interests are considered legitimate and formal channels of communication are available for the articulation of these interests. Once institutionalized, a conflict is more likely to continue as the parties develop a mutual interest in each other's survival (Kahn-Freund 1954, p. 201). Thus, institutionalization does not resolve a conflict, in the sense of eliminating it.

In the paradigm under discussion, institutionalization was taken as an independent variable of the intensity and militancy of a conflict. Since institutionalization involves recognizing or legitimizing the contending parties and developing methods to deal with various issues as they arise, we can hypothesize that though the intensity of a conflict over a particular issue is likely to lessen as demands are acknowledged and rules developed, a minimum level of intensity will persist so long as the parties remain intact. In contrast, we would expect institutionalization strongly to affect militancy. Militant strategy aims for recognition of demands which, once met, reduces militant activity. These relations are expressed in Table 29.

In order to observe the operation and effects of institutionalization in an empirical setting, it was necessary to specify the components of the concept and suitable indicators. At the empirical level, institutionalization refers to:

1. a mutual recognition of the legitimacy of each party;
2. a mutual recognition of the legitimacy of the claims of each party; and
3. available and mutually acceptable channels of communication for dealing with interests and claims.

Table 29

Influence of Institutionalization on Intensity and Militancy

Low Level of Institutionalization	High Level of Institutionalization
1. Intensity High Militancy High	2. Intensity High Militancy Low
3. Intensity Low Militancy High	4. Intensity Low Militancy Low

The presence of conflict agents as previously defined was taken as an indicator of components two and three. Legal acts, such as legislation and court decisions, also attested to the presence or absence of mutual recognition. The recognition of claims was inferred from documents and activities which implicitly or explicitly indicated that agreements had been reached or negotiations commenced.

Throughout our description of the Catholic and French school situations, we noted the shifting of the levels of intensity and militancy in response to increasing and decreasing levels of institutionalization. Catholic schools were explicitly recognized or legitimized in the Scott Act of 1863 and in the British North

America Act, and Catholic members of the government and the legislature acted as conflict agents.

As education became increasingly important, the problem of financing under existing agreements and the desire to extend Catholic schools to the secondary level became more salient. Existing agreements had to be challenged, but in so doing the visibility of the issue was increased and the opposition perceived a threat to its position. This placed a heavy strain on the delicate balance of legitimacy achieved through previous arrangements.

As the situation moved into the thirties, the intensity had increased considerably and the level of militancy started to climb, though kept in check through a continuing minimum level of institutionalization. Nevertheless, the whole system of regulation was in danger of collapse as the contenders struggled over the very legitimacy of Catholic schools, no longer dealing with lower-level issues within an accepted framework of recognition and mediation.

By 1936, certain concessions indicated a partial recognition of Catholic claims and seemed to guarantee the continued existence of Catholic schools, even though under considerable financial strain. A salaried official was appointed to deal with the government on behalf of Catholic interests and the government found the means to handle some of the financial problems through departmental rather than legislative action. Slowly, new legislation was introduced, but always avoided direct reference to Catholic schools. During the 1960's, the process commenced again, culminating in the 1971 elections.

French schooling followed a similar pattern. In practice, French schools were recognized up to Confederation and a system of conflict agents had developed, especially through the use of the dual inspectorate. Though Ontario continued implicitly to recognize these schools, they were not considered in the British North America Act. Gradually, as we saw, the legitimacy of French schools was challenged, concluding with Regulation 17. The regulation reduced the degree of recognition previously in effect and reduced the effectiveness of the dual inspectorate. Correspondingly, the level of intensity increased, as did the level of militant activity. In effect, Regulation 17 de-institutionalized the conflict. Militancy less-

ened as it became apparent that Regulation 17 would be modified through negotiation. The intensity remained at a relatively high level until the new arrangements were well established and the interests of Francophones turned to Catholic
schooling.

We examined the operation of the complex system of
conflict agents which developed as a result of the modification
of Regulation 17. Inspectors, principals and vice-principals,
along with board members in Tecumseh, functioned to deal
with and control local issues arising over the operation of
French classes. In 1968 the government responded relatively
quickly with little opposition to the demands made in the early
sixties. The increasing intensity and militancy following this
legislation is interesting. Regarding institutionalization, the
legislation legitimized French schools as such and provided for
additional institutional means for their development.
However, this served to open the issue at the local community
level and, where secondary schools were concerned, put the
demands of Francophones in a system which had not
previously developed institutional means for their mediation.
This leads us to a consideration of a class of variables which
could appropriately be termed community variables.

At the local level, the most obvious factors that would
have considerable bearing on the topic are demographic.
Communities can be described according to the way in which
certain characteristics of their populations are distributed. At
one extreme, a municipality in Ontario without a Francophone
population would hardly experience conflict between
Francophones and Anglophones at the local level; nor, at the
other extreme, would a municipality in which only
Francophones resided.

Communities of the above type may find themselves involved in conflicts at the regional or provincial level. This was
the case in Tecumseh during the events leading up to
Regulation 17, when the town was basically French and
Catholic. It faced, as a total community, a hostile external environment. The character of the conflict in Tecumseh began to
change as its population changed. These changes affected the
situation in two ways. Firstly, the proportion of Anglophones
gradually increased so that Tecumseh Francophones had to

deal with the opposition internally as well as externally. Apart from the extreme cases, the proportion of each category will have some bearing on local conflicts. Indeed, a certain number of both groups is required in order to generate locally based social categories or collectivities. To see the relation between proportion and intensity, one need only compare Essex County, with 8.5 percent of its population reporting French as their mother tongue, to Nipissing (Sturgeon Falls) with 32.8 percent, and the Stormont-Dundas-Glengary region (Cornwall) with 30.7 percent (Census of Canada 1971).

Secondly, it is also important to consider the religious dimension. In Tecumseh, insofar as elementary schooling was concerned, conflict over language of instruction did not become a local issue until sufficient English Catholics were included in the population to generate a social category. English Protestants in Tecumseh simply did not come into contact with Francophones over school issues. The whole history of French-English conflict was therefore played out locally within the parish and its related institutions. English Protestants only came into contact with Francophones in the sixties when the issue moved to the secondary school level, but even there it was at the county rather than the local community level. Locally then, the conflict took on some of the characteristics of a family quarrel with all the interpersonal bitterness that accompanies conflict between people closely tied together (Coser 1956, pp. 60-65).

At the same time, the presence of English Catholics placed a check on intensity. From the perspective of individuals and their commitments to roles, English and French Catholics in Tecumseh were subjected to certain cross-pressures. An English Catholic was open to the interests and pressures of English versus French Canadians. As a Catholic, s/he had a commitment to Catholic interests which were shared with Francophones and opposed to Protestant interests, the proponents of which were almost totally Anglophone. The English Catholic, therefore, formed a connecting link between English Protestant and French Catholic on all but the school issue. Another factor may be introduced here. In our consideration of significant issues in Tecumseh in 1966, a set of general issues apart from French-English and Catholic-Protestant conflict was noted. These were referred to as community issues. It was suggested that if these issues were sufficiently attractive, whether people were French or English, Protestant or Catholic, they would be drawn together into other systems. This suggests a variable which has received considerable attention in the literature. It refers to the extent to which obligations and memberships criss-cross over several social categories in the life of the community (Coleman 1957, p. 22; Coser 1956, p. 78; Williams 1964, p. 369; Dahrendorf 1959, p.213; Gluckman 1963, pp. 1-4; Galtung 1966 p. 149). A considerable number of criss-crossing memberships will check the extent to which many individuals can commit themselves to categories involved in a given conflict system, thereby moderating the level of intensity. This is incorporated into our schema in Table 30.

Table 30
Influence of Institutionalization and Criss-Crossing
Memberships on Intensity and Militancy

	Low Level of Institutionalization	High Level of Institutionalization
Little Criss-crossing	1. Intensity High Militancy High	2. Intensity High Militancy Low
Extensive Criss-crossing	3. Intensity Low Militancy High	4. Intensity Low Militancy Low

A final factor suggested by the Tecumseh data, to which I have already referred, is the autonomy of local systems. The concepts of vertical and horizontal patterns of organization provided a useful means for dealing with the problem of the erosion of locally based authority on key issues. A community's vertical pattern is defined as "the structural and functional relations of its various social units and sub-systems to extra-

196

community systems" (Warren 1963, p. 161). Horizontal patterns refer to "the structural and functional relations of various social units and sub-systems to each other " (Warren 1963, p. 162).

If the horizontal pattern is weak, that is, if decisions concerning issues crucial to the community require the intervention of the vertical system, then the interest-articulating activity of local conflict agents and agencies will take place in extra-local systems. The actual confrontation will, in this case, take place in Toronto or some regional centre rather than in Tecumseh. Agents and agencies located elsewhere will carry on the conflict, with little need for the involvement of local citizens *in relation to each other*. Thus, the stronger the horizontal pattern on a given issue, the greater the possibility of an intense conflict at the local level.

The general trend over the period covered in Chapter 6 was toward an increasing weakening of the horizontal pattern of organization. Nevertheless, at different periods and given variations in the character of particular issues, the role of local units in relation to each other varied in both directions. The decision to create a separate school district or to introduce French classes or schools remains, for the most part, a local prerogative. However, the limits placed on these systems in contrast with public and Anglophone schools dictated that decisions on future development were a prerogative of the vertical system. To extend Catholic schooling to the secondary level or to increase the revenue of separate school boards were issues which had to be dealt with at the provincial level. Protestant and Catholic seldom confronted each other locally over Catholic schooling.

There was another aspect of this dimension. Those organizations which I identified as conflict agencies had themselves tended toward centralization, eroding the contribution of local branches. During the mid-sixties, Tecumseh Catholics through their C.P.T.A.'s could do little more than discuss issues and make recommendations to regional and provincial offices. This was, of course, mainly due to the fact that the decisions required to meet Catholic demands had to be made in Toronto, not Tecumseh. But it was also due to the "branch plant" orientation of large scale voluntary associations. To understand this, we need only contrast the mid-sixties with the thirties. A surge of local activity followed the bishops' decision to involve the laity in the struggle for Catholic schools. Massive campaigns defined the issues, and provided the means for extensive local participation. Decisions about goals and strategies required local input; local intensity increased under the combined effect of decreasing institutionalization and strengthening of the horizontal pattern. Ironically, the agencies generated during this period themselves centralized; executive committees simply replaced bishops. The disappearance of the C.P.T.A.'s in Tecumseh in the seventies was partly due to the apathy generated by this process.

The conflict over French schooling followed a somewhat different course. Until the forties Tecumseh was, for all practical purposes, a French Catholic community. Internal conflict insofar as these issues were concerned was absent. Nevertheless, the intensity was high during the events surrounding Regulation 17 when the town as a *total unit* confronted the vertical system. Until 1968, the establishment and operation of French classes within Tecumseh schools was a local matter. This served to maintain a certain level of intensity as French Catholic confronted English Catholic. The 1968 legislation further institutionalized the situation, but left the question of secondary schooling to local boards. It was over secondary schooling that the intensity increased after 1968 as French-language advisory committees clashed with county and regional public school boards.

Francophone agencies then pressured the government to remove decision on this right, as it was defined, out of the horizontal system in order to guarantee French secondary schooling where appropriate and reduce the possibility of local conflicts. The 1972 Ministerial Commission recognized this problem:

> The Commission wishes, in fact, to affirm its belief in the value and importance of the principle of local autonomy in education. It notes, that this principle must he reconciled in reasonable ways with the responsibility of the province to ensure that fair and equitable treatment is given to the official language

minority and that no board acts in an unjust and arbitrary manner against the needs and wishes of this minority.
(Ministerial Commission 1972, pp. 21-22)

By 1973, taking all factors into consideration, Tecumseh had reached a state best characterized by cell four, Table 31. During the seventies, it is true that the level of intensity increased slightly in response to the secondary school question, and may continue to increase if Francophones move to establish a composite French language elementary school as they seemed to be preparing to do. This will move the situation closer to cell two, but the level of intensity will be held in check by a fairly extensive criss-crossing of loyalties.

This, then, is proposed as a paradigm for the analysis of community conflict. The total paradigm evolved out of the research itself, out of an interaction between the literature on social conflict, the data collected in Tecumseh, and my own thinking and values. To test its efficacy requires comparative studies of several communities.

Conflict and Assimilation

Professor Coser, in his consideration of the functions of social conflict through analysis of the work of Georg Simmel, discussed a widely accepted proposition on the formation and persistence of social groups. He noted that:

Conflict sets boundaries between groups within a social system by strengthening group consciousness and awareness of separateness, thus establishing the identity of groups within the system.
(Coser 1956, p.34)

Earlier we discussed forces of association and dissociation, looking at the way in which the categories of language and religion divide people at the local level. The resulting formation of social categories was posited as one of the conditions for conflict relations. The intensity of a conflict situation was defined in terms of increasing involvement of category

199

members through conflict agencies. In other words, the greater the intensity of a conflict, the stronger the boundaries between the participating groups and the greater the extent to which the participants identify with these groups.

Table 31
Schematic Presentation of Variables for the Analysis of
Community Conflict

	Low Level of Institutionalization	High Level of Institutionalization	
Little Criss- crossing	1. Intensity High Militancy High	2. Intensity High Militancy Low	Strong Horizontal Pattern
Extensive Criss- crossing	3. Intensity Low Militancy High	4. Intensity Low Militancy Low	Weak Horizontal Pattern

The extent to which a conflict becomes institutionalized plays an interesting role in boundary maintenance. First, institutionalization controls the level of militancy and, to a certain extent, modifies intensity. However, insofar as institutionalization involves the legitimation of the participating parties and their interests, it contributes to a continuity of the parties, of collective boundaries and corresponding identities. The kinds of social categories with which this work has dealt were based on nationality, language, and religion. It is these kinds of groupings to which the concept of assimilation is generally applied. A simple translation, from the vocabulary of assimilation to the vocabulary of conflict suggests that a highly intense conflict reduces the level of assimilation and that an institutionalized conflict mitigates the force of assimilation.

To appreciate fully the relationship between assimilation and conflict, it is necessary to introduce a conceptual

A Paradigm for the Analysis

distinction which has become fairly common in the literature on assimilation. I refer to the distinction between cultural and structural assimilation. The distinction has been made by a number of scholars working in this area (Breton 1964; Eisenstadt 1954; Gordon 1964; Rosenthal 1960; Vallée 1957). Milton Gordon refers to "cultural or behavioural assimilation" and "structural assimilation." The former is defined as the extent to which members of one ethnic group take on the beliefs, values, and general cultural patterns of another; the latter, as the extent to which members of one group participate in the "cliques, clubs, and institutions of the host society" (Gordon 1964, p. 71). Eisenstadt advances a similar distinction between "acculturation," which refers to "the extent to which the immigrant learns various roles, norms, and customs of the absorbing society" and "institutional dispersion," referring to "the migrant group as such, and its place in the social structure of the absorbing society" (Eisenstadt 1954, pp. 12-13). Raymond Breton's concept of "institutional completeness" is similar to Gordon's "structural assimilation" and Eisenstadt's "institutional dispersion" (Breton 1964).

This study, insofar as it has dealt with the development and maintenance of social categories, incorporates the notion of structural assimilation and its opposite, structural separation. To return to the conflict variables, institutionalization, though maintaining a certain level of structural separation, would promote cultural assimilation in that it solidifies lines of contact and communication. I might add that conflict itself requires contact and communication and therefore contributes to cultural assimilation. However, a conflict in which high levels of intensity and militancy are exhibited would at least retard, perhaps reverse, the process of structural assimilation. Thus, those factors which contribute to the intensity and militancy of a conflict also retard the process of structural assimilation.

Any factor which serves to increase the visibility of a particular issue in a conflict will also potentially influence the process of structural assimilation. Also, the centralizing tendency of large scale voluntary associations, by promoting a weakening of the horizontal system, contributes to a modification of intensity at the local level, and permits

201

structural assimilation. More concretely, the desire of Franco-Ontarian conflict agencies to remove from local school boards decisions on the creation of French schools reduces the intensity of local conflicts. This, in turn, stimulates structural assimilation. But, few would be prepared consciously to stimulate local conflict in order to maintain group boundaries.

The efficacy of the conflict model is that it permits one to capture the reality of boundary-maintenance activity, and of people responding to historical forces of association and dissociation. The emphasis is on interaction and intergroup relations. In contrast, assimilation studies, which stress the measurement of individuals' attributes as indices of assimilation, fail to capture the collective base of intergroup relations, and stress the problems of one or another party abstracted from the relationships between parties.

Tecumseh, Ontario

Francophones as a collectivity have maintained a tenuous hold in Tecumseh despite the overwhelming Anglophone influence. Using language as an index, we saw that Tecumseh Francophones, though not as strong as their confreres in the Ottawa Valley and northeastern Ontario, have maintained an amazing viability against the extreme pressure of anglicization in the Detroit-Windsor metropolitan complex. It was when we focused on interaction and institutional patterns that we saw the categories of language and religion being arranged and re-arranged over time and according to the issues of the moment.

The linguistic and religious categories have meaning only in an historical context. They are important in Tecumseh because of French-English and Catholic-Protestant contacts and the nature of those contacts throughout Canada. Tecumseh presented us with one local expression of a national drama. The dialogue and the conflict continues at the federal and provincial levels of social organization, but insofar as the consequences affect people's daily lives, they are played out at the local or community level of social organization. The church which Tecumseh citizens attend, the organizations to which they belong, the people with whom they interact, the school to which they send their children and the interests which they consider worth defending are all influenced by the historical fact of French-English relations in Canada.

In studies of this nature, the individual is necessarily lost as one considers positions, roles, and collectivities. There is a certain danger, therefore, in forgetting or perhaps just ignoring the fact that it is individuals who are affected by and affect the dynamics of the collective experience. There are many Francophones in their late fifties and sixties in Tecumseh who attended school during the time Regulation 17 was in force. Their skills in reading and writing in French are quite limited, far more so than those who attended school before or after the modification of that regulation. There are English Catholics in their late forties who were sent to the public school because "the separate school was too French." These experiences influence later interaction patterns, values and opinions.

The problem of identity is great. Consider a child who is brought up during the first ten years of his or her life in a decidedly French atmosphere. One's mother tongue becomes part of one's conception of oneself. S/he soon begins to learn as S/he attends French classes in a predominantly English school that in some way his or her identity is inferior to that of the others; all the important things are done in the other language. Who then is s/he? If s/he is a child of working-class parents, s/he will probably adopt the other identity since work is done in English. S/he will not have had the opportunity to read French literature and perhaps the French press at home; if s/he attends high school s/he may or may not enroll in French classes. A middle-class child might well follow the same route, but it is equally possible s/he will follow the other route as s/he is encouraged by parents and teachers to be French. There is no danger s/he will not learn English, but the middle-class route of organizations and participation may keep him or her within those institutional arrangements that support the continuity of the collectivity. Whatever his or her class origins, identity will be problematic. It will be even more problematic when the child realizes that historically neither s/he nor his/her people are immigrants, but subordinates in a country they call their own.

As I write these last few words, the Government of Quebec has tabled Bill 22 in the National Assembly. Bill 22 de-

clares French the official language of the province, extending
its use in education, commerce, public services, legal institutions, and the professions. This action is yet another manifestation of two centuries of French-English conflict. Allowing for
obvious variations by province and community, it must be
viewed in the same context of relationships as Tecumseh or
Sturgeon Falls, Ontario; Moncton, New Brunswick; or St.
Boniface, Manitoba. Behind the new Quebec legislation are the
same motives as those which stimulated reaction against the
restrictions on French at the time of the conquest and attempt
to preserve a language and a way of life on an overwhelmingly
Anglophone continent. This statement is made with a full
awareness of the numerical majority of French speakers in the
Province of Quebec.

The Act will be seen as a threat to the status of the
English language and institutions. Objectively, the Act does
carry such a threat, but the status which English has enjoyed
vis-à-vis French in Quebec cannot be compared to the status
held by the French language in Ontario before Regulation 17.
It is true that Ontario has passed relatively progressive
legislation on the status of French in education since 1968.
But the French language does not possess the same status in
Ontario public life as English has in Quebec.

The pattern which reactions are likely to follow were
apparent the day Bill 22 was tabled. The Parti québécois will
oppose the bill on the ground that it provides insufficient
protection for French (*Le Jour*, Montreal, May 22, 1974).
Anglophones will also oppose the bill on the grounds that it is a
threat to the status of English and English institutions.
English Catholic and English Protestant educational organizations early expressed their disapproval and fears (*The Gazette*,
Montreal, May 22, 1974). The bill will undoubtedly be tested
in the courts. The Quebec Anglophone press in May, 1974 read
like the Franco-Ontarian press between 1910 and 1914, only
the language had changed. Official bilingualism appears to be
an objective held only by Francophones outside Quebec and
Anglophones within Quebec. It is not likely that Québécois will
favour bilingualism since Canadians have shown little interest
in it since 1867.

Epilogue

The struggle continues. The trends pointed to in the first edition have held. The development of residential land during the ensuing decade opened Tecumseh to a significantly large in-migration of Anglophones, thus limiting the ability of the "old village" to maintain Francophone institutions and a visible use of French in everyday life. Nevertheless a remarkable tenacity remained. Taking the retention indices as evidence, between 1971 and 1981 Tecumseh dropped 12 points on the F.M.T. index, Windsor remained the same, suggesting an in-migration of Francophones from Tecumseh and the surrounding rural areas as well as from further afield. Essex and Kent Counties dropped by 2 points. On the more sensitive F.S.H. index Tecumseh dropped 12 points but remained higher than either Windsor or Essex and Kent.

Putting this in the context of Ontario as a whole, the situation remained surprisingly stable over the decade between 1971 and 1981 with the proportions of those reporting "French Mother Tongue" and "French Spoken at Home" decreasing by less than one percent. With regard to selected regions, Eastern Ontario exhibited significant increases while Northeastern and Southwestern Ontario decreased slightly on both indicators. Though the trends follow Richard Joy's "bilingual belt" thesis (1972), one must allow for the influx of French-speakers into the Ottawa-Carleton region in response to the federal policies on bilingualism and the influence of this fact on the province-wide language profile.

One may adopt either a pessimistic or an optimistic view of these trends. An optimistic view would stress the observation that French language communities have maintained themselves and a significant French presence has held in the Province as a whole in spite of the overwhelming force of English in the market place, in entertainment, and in the media. The observation may be explained with reference to the accommodations made over the past two decades. The Ontario Secondary Schools and Boards of Education Amendment Act and the Schools Administration Act of 1968 finally gave full legitimacy to French language schools in the Province, an objective for which Franco-Ontarians had fought since the 1880's. The federal Official Languages Act of 1968-69 and its accompanying programmes supporting "official language minorities" further legitimated the use of French. To this we can add Ontario's recent Bill 8 extending French language services in the public domain. Each of these legislative measures has increased the level of institutionalization between the two parties and, though ensuring their continuity, has reduced the intensity and militancy of the struggle.

A pessimistic view would hold that this, in turn, weakens group boundaries, opening Franco-Ontario communities to further deterioration. But there remains a counterforce, the "English backlash" which, insofar as it prompts a militant response from the other side, will perhaps do more to maintain French language communities than to destroy them.

During the 1987 summer election Ontario witnessed an exceptionally clamorous backlash. Bill 8 had been passed prior to the election with agreement from all parties in the legislature. It wasn't until the Conservative leader questioned the implications of the legislation in the subsequent election campaign that the backlash occurred. Bilingualism in Ontario became the "hidden election issue." Under the encouragement of the Alliance for the Preservation of English in Canada, allegedly 7,000 strong in Ontario, several townships and counties in Eastern Ontario voted to request a referendum to repeal Bill 8. Bill 8 remained intact, but one might expect the Ontario Government to proceed very cautiously with its implementation.

Quebec's language legislation announcing French as the official language and the opposition of Quebec Anglophones was frequently cited by the Alliance for the Preservation of English in Canada and its supporters as the principal rationale for its position. In contrast, Franco-Ontarians have referred to the status of English in Quebec as a rationale for their demands. The latter are closer to actual linguistic practices in Quebec. Quebecer's receive all federal services in the language of their choice. In practice English Quebecers receive provincial services in English, at times only if requested, but mainly as a matter of goodwill. Such services are more likely to be found in regions where the Anglophone population is of sufficient size to warrant them. Ontario's Bill 8 does no more with respect to the French language than is the current practice in Quebec with respect to English.

In addition, a child of English-speaking Canadian parents may attend school from daycare to university in English. It is possible, in Montreal and surrounding regions, for a child to grow up without a knowledge of French, and many do. On the other hand, Bill 101 gave French predominance, and as a result, it is the English-speakers who are becoming bilingual as French-speakers in Ontario have been for the past century. Specific articles in Bill 101 have been and are being challenged in the courts. Presently regulations governing the use of languages other than French on commercial signs are before the Supreme Court of Canada. The Anglophone position in this debate has been articulated by Alliance Quebec and several regional associations partially funded by the federal government's "official language minority" programmes.

The federal discourse on language, based as it is on a vision of a bilingual/bicultural Canadian nation, equates the position of Quebec Anglophones with Francophones outside of Quebec as "official language minorities." The use of the term "minority" frequently confuses numbers with power. Franco-Ontarians and Quebec Anglophones are minorities relative to the majority languages in each province. But what about the intersection of language and power? Do Franco-Ontarians as a category possess the same economic and political power as anglophone Quebecers? Are Anglophones Quebecers perhaps less of a minority on this dimension? Furthermore the concept of official language minorities ignores the context in which various languages come to have predominance over others. The crucial issue is the linguistic reference group for Anglophones or Francophones outside or inside Quebec. Table 32 is an attempt to relate the federal official language discourse to linguistic reference groups.

Looked at this way, Anglophones in Canada as a whole are an official language majority within a linguistic majority setting. Quebec Anglophones are an official language minority, but in relation to Canada and North America are in reality a majority. English in Quebec is under little threat. Conversely, Quebec Francophones, though an official language majority, in relation to Canada and North America are a minority. French in Quebec is under threat. Francophones outside of Quebec are officially and contextually a minority. Quebec's language policies must be understood in this light, its objective is not to threaten English but to maintain itself, a project which cries out for support from Anglophones in the Province.

Table 32
Federal Discourse and Linguistic Reference Group
(Canada & North America)

Official Languages Discourse	Majority	Minority
Majority	Anglophones in Canada	Quebec Francophones
Minority	Quebec Anglophones	Francophones Outside of Quebec

The issue is, of course, more complex than a discussion of languages alone reveals. Intersecting with the language question are competing visions of Canada and Quebec and the relation between the two. The Quebec vision is based on the concept of dual nationhood, however this is to be expressed constitutionally (i.e., as sovereignty-association or as two nations within a single state), while the federal language policies are based on the concept of a pan-Canadian, single nation-state. The status of the two languages becomes a major symbol around which these two visions are expressed.

The Catholic school question in Ontario is no less complex. In 1984 the Ontario Government under William Davis announced, with support from the three parties in the legislature, that full-funding would be extended to grades 11 through 13 in the Province's separate school system. The reaction was much stronger than the reaction to Bill 8. The Anglican Archbishop, Lewis Garnsworthy, accused Mr. Davis of "Hitler-like" tactics. During the 1985 election Frank Miller (the new Tory leader following the resignation of Mr. Davis) and William Davis were victims of militant protesters throughout the campaign and were frequently labeled "fascist" or "Hitler" as they attempted to defend the policy. The new Liberal led minority government maintained the decision to implement the policy. The decision is now before the courts.

The opposition has centered its argument in the call for a universal and secular public educational system based upon the separation of church and state. Two other positions have quickly attached themselves to the rhetoric of a universal system. One is the anti-papist attitude buried deeply in the Ontario Protestant mind, a position frequently linked with the anti-French movement, and the other is the fear of teachers in the public system of losing jobs. The Ontario Secondary School Teachers Federation, public school boards, and the Protestant churches have mounted a militant campaign against the policy. It would be an error however to assume a lack of overlapping social categories on this issue. A proportion of Franco-Ontarians as well as English Catholics, especially in the metropolitan regions, support a universal and secular system as does a large proportion of the citizenry of Quebec. On the other hand, if such a system were to be established in Ontario, one might speculate that the Protestant anti-papists would oppose the move. Their objective is not to separate church and state but to eliminate the funding of Roman Catholic separate schools.

Bibliography

Books and Articles

Arès, Richard. "La grande pitié de nos minorité française." *Relations* 267 (1963).

Bernard, Jessie. *The Sociology of Community*. Glencoe, Ill.: Scott, Foresman, 1973.

Blais, Louis. "Study of the Viability of French-Canadian Populations Outside of the Province of Quebec." Unpublished paper. Carleton University, Ottawa, 1969.

Blishen, Bernard, R. "The Construction and Use of an Occupational Class Scale." In *Canadian Society: Sociological Perspectives*, edited by B.R. Blishen et al. New York: Free Press, 1961.

_____. "Social Class and Opportunity in Canada." *Canadian Review of Sociology and Anthropology* 7 (1970): 110-127.

Brault, Lucien. *Bref exposé de l'enseignement bilingue au XXe siècle dans l'Ontario et les autres provinces*. Kingston, Ont.: Collège Militaire Royal, 1966.

Breton, Raymond. "Institutional Completeness of Ethnic Communities and the Personal Relations of Immigrants." *American Journal of Sociology* 70 (1964): 193-205.

Brunet, Michel, *La présence anglaise et les Canadiens*: Montréal: Beauchemin, 1964.

Bruyn, Severyn T. *The Human Perspective in Sociology*. Englewood Cliffs, N.J.: Prentice-Hall, 1966.

Caldwell, Gary & Waddell, Eric. *The English of Quebec: From Majority to Minority Status*. Québec: Institut québécois de recherche sur la culture, 1982.

Chauvin, F.-X. "Les Canadiens-français d'Essex et de Kent." *Relations* 72 (1946): 365-369.

Cicourel, Aaron V. *Method and Measurement in Sociology*. New York: Free Press, 1964.

Clark, S.D. *The Developing Canadian Community*. Toronto: University of Toronto Press, 1962.

Coleman, James C. *Community Conflict*. New York: Free Press, 1957.

Coons, W.H. et al. (eds.). *The Individual, Language and Society in Canada*. Ottawa: The Canada Council, 1977.

Coser, Lewis A. *The Functions of Social Conflict*. New York: Free Press, 1956.

Dahrendorf, Ralf. *Class and Class Conflict in Industrial Society*. Stanford, Calif.: Stanford University Press, 1959.

Drake, St. Clair. "Some Observations on Interethnic Conflict as One Type of Intergroup Conflict." *Journal of Conflict Resolution* 1 (1957): 162.

Dubin, Robert. "Industrial Conflict and Social Welfare." *Journal of Conflict Resolution* 1 (1957): 187.

Community & Conflict

Eisenstadt, S.N. *The Absorption of Immigrants*. London: Routledge and Kegan Paul, 1954.

Farrell, J.K.A. "The History of the Roman Catholic Church in London, Ontario, 1826-1931." Master's thesis, University of Western Ontario, 1949.

Galtung, John. "Rank and Social Integration: A Multidimensional Approach." In *Sociological Theories in Progress*, edited by Joseph Berger et al., pp. 145-198. Boston: Houghton Mifflin, 1966.

Garigue, Philippe. "The French Canadian Family." In *Canadian Dualism*, edited by Mason Wade, pp. 181-201. Toronto: University of Toronto Press, 1960.

Gluckman, Max. *Custom and Conflict in Africa*. Oxford: Basil Blackwell, 1963.

Gold, Gerald L. "Voluntary Associations and a New Economic Elite in a French-Canadian Town." In *Communities and Culture in French Canada*, edited by Gerald L. Gold and Marc-Adélard Tremblay, pp. 202-217. Toronto: Holt, Rinehart and Winston, 1973.

Gold, Raymond L. "Roles in Sociological Field Observations." *Social Forces* 36 (1958).

Gordon, Milton M. *Assimilation in American Life*. New York: Oxford University Press, 1964.

Gould, Julius, and Kolb, William L. *A Dictionary of the Social Sciences*. New York: Free Press, 1964.

Harris, Chauncy D., and Ullman, E.L. "The Nature of Cities." In *Cities and Society*, edited by Paul K. Hatt and Albert J. Reiss. Glencoe, Ill.: Free Press, 1951.

Helling, Rudolf, and Boyce, Edward. *A Demographic Survey of Essex County and Metropolitan Windsor*. London, Ont.: The Diocese of London, 1965.

Hodge, G.D. and Qadeer, M.A. *Towns and Villages in Canada*. Toronto: Butterworth, 1983.

Horowitz, Irving L. "Concensus, Conflict and Cooperation: A Sociological Inventory." *Social Forces* 41 (1963): 183.

Hughes, Everett C. *French Canada in Transition*. Chicago: University of Chicago Press, 1943.

_____, and Hughes, Helen MacGill. *Where People Meet: Racial and Ethnic Frontiers*. Glencoe, Ill.: Free Press, 1952.

Joy, Richard J. *Languages in Conflict*. Carleton Library No. 61. Toronto: McClelland and Stewart, 1972.

Juteau-Lee, Danielle & Jean Lapointe. "Indentité culturelle et identité structurelle dans l'Ontario francophone: analyse d'une transition." *Actes du IIIᵉ colloque consacré a l'identité culturelle et la francophonie dans les Amériques*. Québec: Centre international de recherche sur le bilingualisme, 1978.

Kahn-Freund, O. "Intergroup Conflicts and their Settlement." *British Journal of Sociology* 5 (1954): 201.

Lajeunesse, E.J. *The Windsor Border Region*. Toronto: Ryerson, 1960.

Bibliography

Lapalme, Victor. "Les Franco-Ontariens et la politique provincial." Master's thesis, Université d'Ottawa, 1968.

Lower, Arthur R.M. *Canadians in the Making*. Toronto: Longmans, Green, 1958.

Mack, Raymond W., and Snyder, Richard C. "The Analysis of Social Conflict: Toward an Overview and Synthesis." *Journal of Conflict Resolution* 1 (1957): 218.

Maheu, Robert. *Les Francophones du Canada, 1941-1991*. Montréal: Editions Parti Pris, 1970.

McKinney, John C. *Constructive Typology and Social Theory*. New York: Appleton-Century-Crofts, 1966.

McLeod-Arnopoulos, Sheila. *Voices From French Ontario*. Montreal: McGill-Queens University Press, 1982.

Merton, Robert K. *Social Theory and Social Structure*. Rev. ed. New York: Free Press, 1957.

Morrison, N.F. *Garden Gateway to Canada*. Toronto: Ryerson, 1954.

Nisbet, Robert A. *The Quest for Community*. New York: Oxford University Press, 1953.

Ollivier, Maurice. *British North America Acts and Selected Statutes, 1867-1962*. Ottawa: Queen's Printer, 1962.

Ouellet, Fernand. "Les fondements historiques de l'option séparatiste dans le Québec." *Canadian Historical Review* 42 (1962): 185-203.

Park, Robert E. *Race and Culture*. New York: Free Press, 1964.

_____, and Burgess, Ernest W. *Introduction to the Science of Sociology*. Chicago: University of Chicago Press, 1921.

Parsons, Talcott, *The Social System*. New York: Free Press, 1951.

_____. "Social Class and Class Conflict in the Light of Recent Sociological Theory." In *Essays in Sociological Theory*, edited by Talcott Parsons. Rev. ed. New York: Free Press, 1954.

Porter, John. *The Vertical Mosaic*. Toronto: University of Toronto Press, 1965.

Rosenthal, Erich. "Acculturation without Assimilation." *American Journal of Sociology* 66 (1960): 275-288.

Rudin, Ronald. *The Forgotten Quebecers*. Québec: Institut québécois de recherche sur la culture, 1985.

Ryerson, Stanley B. *The Founding of Canada: Beginnings to 1815*. Toronto: Progress Books, 1963.

_____. *Unequal Union*. New York: International Publishers, 1968.

Schumpeter, Joseph A. *History of Economic Analysis*. New York: Oxford University Press, 1954.

Scott, Frank R. "Areas of Conflict in the Field of Public Law and Policy." In *Canadian Dualism*, edited by Mason Wade. Toronto: University of Toronto Press, 1960.

Seeley, John, et al. *Crestwood Heights*. Toronto: University of Toronto Press, 1956.

Selltiz, Claire, et al. *Research Methods in Social Relations*. Rev. ed. New York: Holt, 1959.

Simpson, G.E., and Yinger, J.M. *Racial and Cultural Minorities*. New York: Harper and Row, 1953.

Sissons, C.B. *Bi-lingual Schools in Canada*. Toronto: Dent, 1917.

Stewart, Alex. "Territorality and Bilingualism: A Note on Jackson's *Community and Conflict*. *Canadian Ethnic Studies* 12 (1980): 103-108.

Tremblay, Marc-Adélard. "The Acadians of Portsmouth: A Study in Culture Change." Ph.D. thesis, Cornell University, Ithaca, N.Y., 1954.

Vallée, Frank G., et al. "Ethnic Assimilation and Differentiation in Canada." *Canadian Journal of Economics and Political Science* 23 (1957): 540-549.

_____, and de Vries, John. "Issues and Trends in Bilingualism in Canada." In *Advances in the Study of Multilingual Societies*, edited by Joshua Fishman. The Hague: Mouton, 1973.

Vidich, A.J., et al. *Reflections on Community Studies*. New York: Wiley, 1964.

Wade, Mason. *The French Canadians 1760-1945*. New York: Macmillan, 1955.

Walker, Franklin. *Catholic Education and Politics in Ontario*. Toronto: Nelson, 1964.

Warner, W. Lloyd, et al. *Yankee City*. Abridged ed. New Haven: Yale University Press, 1963.

Warren, Roland L. *The Community in America*. Chicago: Rand McNally, 1963.

Warriner, Charles K. "Groups are Real: A Reaffirmation." *American Sociological Review* 21 (1956): 549-554.

Weber, Max. "Class, Status and Power." In *Class, Status and Power*, edited by Reinhard Bendix and Seymour M. Lipset. New York: Free Press, 1953.

Williams, Robin M. Jr. *The Reduction of Intergroup Tensions*. Bulletin 57. New York: Social Science Research Council, 1947.

_____. "Racial and Cultural Relations." In *Review of Sociology: Analysis of a Decade*, edited by J.B. Gittler. New York: Wiley, 1957.

_____. *Strangers Next Door: Ethnic Relations in American Communities*. Englewood Cliffs, N.J.: Prentice-Hall, 1964.

_____. "Social Order and Social Conflict." *American Philosophical Society Proceedings* 114 (1970): 217-225.

_____. "Conflict and Social Order: A Research Strategy for Complex Propositions." *Journal of Social Issues* 28 (1972): 11-26.

Government and Political Party Documents

Communist Party of Canada. "A New Direction for Canada — Defeat the Old Parties." 1963.

Government of Ontario, Department of Economics and Development. *Lake St. Clair Region Economic Survey*. Toronto: Queen's Printer, 1967.

Bibliography

_____, Department of Education. *Instructions 17: English-French Public and Separate Schools*. Toronto: King's Printer, 1913.

_____, Ministry of Education. *Report of Ministerial Commission on French-Language Secondary Education*. Toronto: Queen's Printer, 1972.

_____. *Statutes of the Province of Ontario*. Ch. 121, pp. 533-546, An Act to Amend the Schools Administration Act; Ch. 122, pp. 547-589, An Act to Amend the Secondary Schools and Boards of Education Act. Toronto: Queen's Printer, 1968.

Greater Windsor Industrial Commission. *The Greater Windsor Manufacturers' Directory*. Windsor, 1972.

Liberal Party of Canada. "Liberal Action, October, 1965." 1965.

New Democratic Party. "Resolutions passed by the Third Federal Convention of the New Democratic Party." 1965.

Progressive Conservative Party of Canada. "Policies for People, Policies for Progress." 1965.

Royal Commission on Bilingualism and Biculturalism. *Report*. Book I, "The Official Languages." Ottawa: Queen's Printer, 1967.

_____. *Report*. Book III, "The World of Work." Ottawa: Queen's Printer, 1969.

Statistics Canada. *1961 Census of Canada*. Bulletins CT-16; CX-1; 1.2-9. Ottawa: Queen's Printr, 1961.

_____. *1971 Census of Canada*. Bulletin 1.3-4, Table 20. Ottawa: Queen's Printer, 1972.

_____. *1971 Census Dictionary*. Ottawa: Queen's Printer, 1972.

Town of Tecumseh. Analysis of Real Property and Business Assessment upon which Education Taxes for the Year 1966 will be levied, Schedule 2, 1966.

Newspapers and Associational Records

L'Association canadienne-française d'Education d'Ontario. Rapport de Congrès d'Education canadienne-française d'Ontario. Ottawa, 1910.

_____. Mémoire à la Commission Royale d'Enquête sur le Bilingualisme et Biculturalisme. 1964.

_____. Statuts. Mimeographed. Ottawa: A.C.F.E.O., April, 1965.

_____. *La Vie Franco-Ontarienne*. Vol. 1, 8 (May, 1966); Vol 2, 1 (October, 1966). Ottawa, 1966.

L'Association de Parents et d'Instituteurs de Tecumseh. Minutes of Monthly Meetings. 1956-1966.

Le Conseil supérieur des écoles de langue française. Personal cadre agrée par le Ministère de d'Education d'Ontario et préposé aux écoles de langue française. 1973.

Le Devoir (Montreal). December 19, 1968; August 25, 1969; February 7, 1970.

Le Droit (Ottawa). December 2; December 3, 1965; January 22; May 30, 1966; March 14, September 15, 1973.

English Catholic Education Association of Ontario. *Serving the School with the Cross*. Toronto: 1966.

Essex County Roman Catholic Separate School Board. Charts of the Legislative and Administrative Organization of the Board. Essex, Ontario, 1973.

Evening Record (Windsor). June 1; June 5, 1914.

La Fédération des Associations de Parents et d'Instituteurs de langue française d'Ontario. Règlements et Statuts. Mimeographed. Ottawa: A.P.I., September, 1964.

Federation of Catholic Parent-Teacher Associations of Ontario. Letter to presidents of local associations. September, 1961.

La Fédération des Sociétés St.-Jean-Baptiste d'Ontario. *La Fédération des S.S.J.B. vous offre son service d'entraide*. Ottawa: S.S.J.B., n.d.

La Feuille d'Erable (Tecumseh). April 16; June 4, 1931; May 5; May 12; November 24, 1932; March 30, 1933; December 20, 1934.

The Gazette (Montreal). May 22, 1974.

Le Jour (Montreal). May 22, 1974.

Ontario Separate School Trustees' Association. *The Catholic Trustee*. Toronto: 1936.

Paroisse de Ste-Anne. *Ste-Anne, Mère de Marie*. Tecumseh: Imprimerie LaCasse, 1959.

Pius X Catholic Parent-Teacher Association, Tecumseh. Minutes of Monthly Meetings. 1961-1965.

La Société St-Jean-Baptiste, Tecumseh. Minutes of Monthly Meetings. 1960-1965.

The Star (Toronto). November 9, 1972.

The Star (Windsor). June 14; November 9, 1965; February 22; April 29, 1966; June 28; July 11, 1968; January 23; February 27; March 3; March 27; April 29; May 28; September 9; November 18; December 9, 11, 15, 1969; January 21; March 10, 1970; April 26, 1973.

Tecumseh Catholic Parent-Teacher Association. Minutes of Monthly Meetings. 1954-1965.

Tecumseh Separate School Board. Minutes of Monthly Meetings. December 17, 1927; January 28; April 13, 1928; January 11, 1929; November 8, 1932; December 27, 1935; December 27, 1936; January 6, 1939.

The Tribune (Tecumseh). September 29, 1960; September 22; October 25; December 13, 1962.

Windsor and Essex County French-Language Committees. Brief presented jointly to the Windsor and the Essex County Boards of Education, 1972.